How To Get Rich
Sooner Than You Think!

Volume One

by
Joanna Jordan

All rights reserved under International and Pan-American
Copyright Conventions. Published in the United States by
New Start Publications, Inc., Sterling, Virginia.
Copyright ©1984 by Joanna Jordan
Revised Copyright © by Joanna Jordan 1989

Library of Congress Cataloging in Publication Data
Joanna Jordan

TITLE: How To Get Rich Sooner Than You Think!
Volume One
        I. Title.

ISBN 0-915451-03-4

Manufactured in the United States of America
9 8 7 6 5 4 3 2 1

TABLE OF CONTENTS

The Man And Wife Team Who Decided to Become Rich

Most of the quick to get rich we've heard about in the mail order field won their instant success at least partly by accident. Certainly, they hoped to be rich; certainly, they aimed at that goal as carefully as circumstances allowed. But in many cases the element of chance loomed large, at least in the beginning.

Debra Newton just happened to be inspired by another woman's success. Joan Mazel was motivated mainly by a desire to lose weight. Bob Hagan established his "Frozen Sea Food" mail order company in Miami, Florida, for the only reason; he lived in the area. And so on. Not many of these people made their fast fortunes by brashly and deliberately *planning* to make fast fortunes.

Now meet a man and wife team who did. Their names are Kathy and Daniel Crandall, by training Daniel is a young television producer. They were poor in the late-1970's. It occurred to them one day that they didn't like being poor, and they made a cool, deliberate decision to grow rich. Three years later they were worth an equally cool $2.3 million.

Daniel and Kathy tell their own story here. Having told it, they analyze some of the reasons for their success and mull over the intriguing question of why other men and women succeed —or, as the case may be, fail. As a husband and wife team who succeeded quickly and spectacularly well, they come with excellent credentials. Let's see what we can learn from them.

1

From Rags To Riches In Three Years

Quite literally, we were broke in 1979—and not because we had lost any great fortune. We had never made one. But with my wife, Kathy, we decided to become millionaires.

By 1982 Kathy and I possessed $2.3 million in personal assets.

This took place right here in the United States— and is still taking place— right here in America.

In an era when giant corporations are merging with other giants, you might think the age of opportunities for individuals or small companies is over. It isn't, as our personal experience proves.

Let us tell you how it all started. We had friends making big money. We compared our endeavors. One friend was in the franchise restaurant business, and he would tell us how much money he was making .... One store, then two stores, now he was about to open his third store. Another friend was in the mail order business and he would tell us how much money he was making. The last one got us a little interested and curious and even a little envious in terms of not having all this money to spend that these people enjoyed. My wife would pass along the tales of wealth, telling me about the millions that were made in the mail order field. So we went into the mail order business with that expectation. It was going to be fun. I had nothing to lose except a little time and a few hundred dollars for the initial investment.

We didn't set up any lavish offices or make any major financial commitments. We were simply going to go out and try it and see what happened. We did just that and, lo and behold, we weren't just "playing at it" anymore. We were starting to make some real money.

We became egotistically involved in the challenge of becoming a success in the mail order field. I kept saying to myself what I've said to myself all my life: If someone else can do it, I can do it.

2

It reminded me of the many times when I'd had a rough time in college. I had gone back to school three years after getting out of high school. (U.S. Army Three Years.) I was competing with kids who were very bright and who had come right into college without any three year lapses. It was the same kind of challenge: I wanted A's and B's and I kept thinking, If they can do it, so can I. I'll study hard; I'll read, write, live in the library, do what ever I have to do to succeed.

Even with such determination, the results didn't always hold up. There were geniuses with A averages, and at the time I couldn't maintain one. I found there was more to it than to ask myself, "If someone else can 'cut it', I can too." But it's a sure thing attitude did a lot. I stayed in college, maintained a decent average and got a degree—because, "if the multitude of people can do it, I can too."

I've found it's the same in business. I am not saying that if the chairmen of the board of *Bank America* can be worth a billion dollars, I can too. Or you. To make that much money you have to make a total commitment that is for the most part unrealistic. But I do believe that substantial success, even outstanding success, is not unrealistic but is within the normal scope of endeavor for any man or woman with average ability.

So all I was really saying to myself was, If thousands of people in the United States succeed in business for themselves, *why can't I?* Specifically, if there are mail order companies and if there are individuals who head them successfully, I can be one of that group.

So my wife and I decided to become million-dollar mail order promoters. Our entire asstes consisted of just the two of us. We had no office, no secretary, nothing. We worked out of our home.

Not long after we began, I decided to try and promote digital watches by running small space ads in various magazines. I was determined enough to believe it would happen fast because we were out there with something to say and something to sell and we were competent.

We were bright, but not that talented or creative when it came to business. We just succeeded by one thing "determination." We ran enough advertisements for a long enough

3

period of time so that the law of averages, the law of probability, worked.

The sensible part was that when you have many related products with different exposures, you're better off than [you are with] one advertisement selling the one product.

I just kept telling myself, Well who gives a damn? I'm still a television producer. I can always go back to what I originally was doing. I'm not going to starve. I have no children. My wife can still make a living.

However, that part about my wife making a living was a bit of a fallacy. She found that modeling jobs in Washington, D.C. were quite limited compared with California. At the same time, the purchase of a home, a car and all the things we wanted to have to live comfortably—all these were now piling up into a tremendous drain on us financially. I had to support the business endeavors, too. Just the cost of advertising layouts rendered by commercial artists added up to quite some expense. We were forced to sell our automobile and ride the bus or hitch a ride with friends.

This in-beween period of about four months-when we had our million dollar ambition but very little success-was our time of agony. But we clung to our belief in the law of probability.

My wife and I decided to sell products that were useful. We kept going on the principle that if we ran enough ads in the right publications, that sooner or later we would be a success. (Thank Goodness the Magazines gave us credit.)

The law of probability finally came through for us. We hit on a pocket calculator that we sold for $79 and bought for $12 from Taiwan. In six months we sold 11,000 units. (Nowadays, mail-order companies, are selling the same calculator for $19.95.)

Suddenly our company was a success. We went ahead and found another product then another. We were building a whole line of products— watches, calculators, ceiling fans, pots and pans, knives, art and home accessories.

The line was a winner for us.

It's a psychological fact: Once you've achieved a success— once you've proved you can be a winner— doors open that you couldn't get through before. Other Taiwan companies were now interested in us marketing their products.

4

We sold a hand truck that went great in the Mechanics magazines.

We created a book on how to become a Vegetarian Cook that sold well in the ladies' magazines. We brought in a Real Estate expert and created a whole series of manuals on buying and selling real estate at a profit.

At this point the law of probability was paying off for our company. We weren't a small company anymore. We were hiring professional people for our staff. We spared nothing to get the cream of the crop in creativity and in advertising know-how. We had an in-house advertising agency and a director to handle our buying overseas. Plus an art director with artists working for her, and a full accounting staff.

My wife and I in this expanding corporation felt no compulsion to confine ourselves to any particular kind of product. When we saw something hot and we believed we could make a contribution, we moved fast into that market.

In 1981 we discovered a manufacturer of women's clothing who was a casual friend. He was selling his women's apparel at the rate of $6,000 a month. Not bad, but we could see the women's mail order clothing business was booming, and we felt that with our promotion techniques applied to his excellent craftsmanship, we ought to be able to be very big in the women's apparel business.

That's how the True Quality line of women's fashions began. We talked to a number of experts in the rag trade and finally interested one in joining the company. Then we applied promotion psychology in upgrading and merchandising the creations. In a relatively short time we built a $70,000-a-year business into a $800,000 business.

Meanwhile, we were getting into a direct-mail business: selling household products to holders of credit cards.

My wife and I were only in business a few years, and now we were selling merchandise to credit-card holders at the rate of $2 million a year. It's one of the biggest parts of our business. And it illustrates a truth: One good win gets you other winners.

In turn, this close relationship with such companies opened our eyes to the enormous volume of business that can be transacted via the credit card route. So, again, we found ourselves deciding to prosper from a promotion-oriented type of business that we hadn't, invented. It was another case of acting on an attitude of positive belief: If somebody else can do it and be successful, why can't I?

Let me try and spell out just how I applied this simple approach to get started in multimillion dollar merchandising via credit cards. I reasoned this way: It's not magical. You don't have to be a genius. You don't have to discover or invent the automobile. It's just simple merchandising. It's just following the principle of satisfying peoples' wants.

Selling merchandise by direct mail through the credit-card route is one of the best examples of successful promotional psychology I can show you. Let's take a term out of psychology textbook and apply it to marketing: *frustration level reduction*. People want pleasure, ease, comfort. They don't want problems, irritations, frustrations. They don't want to be made uncomfortable.

Suppose you tell someone, "Look, you can have this fabulous digital watch for only a fraction of its retail value; but what you've got to do is send in your money first, and when your check clears, I'll send you back a notice to come and pick up your digital watch at a specific place at a specific time." That's full of frustrations. You're making it difficult for the customer, as well as vaguely distasteful to him. First of all, you're making him feel uncomfortable about the fact that you don't trust him. Second, he-or-she doesn't understand your instructions. Even if he or she overcomes those two unpleasantnesses, your potential customer still has normal resistance. He or she is not motivated to get up and drive to your store or place of business.

But by selling him with direct mail and letting him pay through the credit-card system, we eliminate all those frustrations. We tell him, "Just say yes if you want this item, and we'll send it directly to your home, postage paid." There's usually an opportunity to try it for 30 days, and then he only pays on a monthly basis as part of the credit card bill, on which he is charging other things, anyway.

Specifically, how did we get into the direct mail credit card merchandise business?

We set it up to work this way: Mastercard, Visa, Carte Blanche and Diners Card has a list of its customers on mailing lists that they rent. We rent the lists and test merchandise such as pots and pans, ceiling fans, and binoculars- items that appeal and are attractive to the majority of the population.

Then we mail out an illustrated brochure to test populace of the credit card holders, offering the item not only at a price that is less than the normal retail price but also the opportunity to purchase the item on their credit card.

If the offer is successful-if a high enough percentage of the people order the item-we then mail the brochure to the entire rest of the list, which usually runs into the millions of people. As soon as an order comes from a customer, our computer immediately mails out the label to our shipping facility and simultaneously bills either the bank or the credit card company.

As for the credit card merchandising business, if you send out good merchandise by mail and the customer can pay it off monthly on a credit card, you're making a practically irresistible offer. Consequently, our results are either astronomical successes or not quite so fabulous successes—but no bombs.

HERE IS WHY PEOPLE FAIL

Surely you agree most people, like you, want success. Who doesn't like to live comfortable? Who doesn't prefer to live in a $500,000-$1,000,000 home, eat appetizing meals served by the butler, be able to buy any type of car you want, take around the world trips— or whatever you enjoy.

All right, then, if everyone wants it, why doesn't everyone have it?

The vast majority of failures are that way because of either or both of two psychological stumbling blocks:
One: Masochism
Two: Insecurity
Now, these aren't just simple phenomena of clear-cut personality types. They vary with the individual, but persons afflicted with them have certain characteristics in common. Let me illustrate these traits in some detail so you can recognize them as enemies to success. A masochistic individual prefers to suffer by not winning. Various experiences in the person's childhood create a desire to be abused or dominated rather than respected. Such individuals feel they must constantly

punish themselves for their guilt from their childhood. They feel low self-esteem, and their punishment manifests itself overtly so that, no matter what they engage in, if [it appears that] a healthy amount of success might come from it, they'll do something to foul it up.

These unfortunates may never realize their problem. It develops on a very subtle level and is mostly subconscious, but they can't bear the idea of succeeding or being completely happy, because that would be contrary to the self-punishment they feel they must infict on themselves.

Masochistic people are those you hear about who had a great opportunity but fouled it up by drinking. Or, if they didn't drink, they gambled. If the didn't gamble, they had all kinds of psychosomatic illnesses. Or they couldn't get up in the morning. Or they blew their business because they [became] cocky. Or maybe they squandered money on nonsensical projects. There are numerous variations of the symptoms, but basically the failure comes from the same perverse motivation: They don't want to succeed.

It isn't always a pure case. For example, he or she may have the dogged determination to bounce back. He may have talent. He may have devised a potentially successful business formula. He goes out, starts to succeed once more, but then fouls himself up all over again.

People do that with marriages. They do that with family and friends. And they do it in-and to-their careers.

The second type of personality problem that keeps many from succeeding is emotional insecurity. Here again the root causes are in childhood experiences. The individual who is afflicted with this difficulty grows up feeling inadequate, inferior, lacking confidence in himself or herself. He doesn't believe he's a person who has ability, who has talent.

Realistically, he or she may have talent, but on a subconscious level he's terribly insecure. As soon as he experiences rejection, which is the norm when you're starting a business or beginning any other enterprise in which you haven't yet made your mark, he or she can't tolerate the rejection. He isn't able to sustain his determination, to keep trying in spite of disappointments, to complete the program or fulfill his or her objective. He's unable to stay with it till the law of probability pays off—to knock on enough doors till at last someone says yes.

He or she can never completely go through that cycle, because it's par for the course that there are more noes than yeses, especially at first. And when he gets a couple of noes, he's destroyed psychologically. He starts rationalizing. He says things to himself like: It won't work. I guess the idea is no good. Oh, well, who has to go into business anyway? Who needs the headaches? I'll take a job, I'll make a living, and I'll be happy....

What he or she is really saying is, Competition is too threatening for me. Rejection is too painful for me. Therefore, I must confine myself to a limited area of function because of my lack of self-confidence and my unwillingness to risk unpleasant experiences for greater rewards.

Those are the two most common internal personality obstacles that prevent people with ability, with an average amount of talent, from pursuing- and winning- a great deal of money by being in business for themselves.

As I implied at the beginning there aren't any 100-percent masochists or insecures. Even the healthiest of us have our doubtful moments.

Anybody can be less of a winner by thinking negatively or thinking too small or thinking-poor. If you start imagining all the reasons you might not succeed in an effort, you can make yourself feel it's not even worth trying. You can form an absolute habit of not winning by not trying.

If you don't remember anything else, remember this: Apply the law of averages. Believe in the law of probabilty. It is not a myth or superstition. It is a mathematical phenomenon. If you have a good idea and you present it to enough of the right people, sooner or later someone will buy. So send out your brochures. Brush off the rejections and keep on advertising.

Suddenly— sooner or later— someone, somewhere will say. You're a winner.

Chapter 1

A "One-Lady or Man" Mail Order Business and How Much You Can Expect to Make from It

If you regularly thumb through one or more magazines a month, you no doubt have been impressed by the rather bewildering array of mail order offers which shout their merits from every page.

Literally everything from diet plans to homebuilding is being successfully sold by mail. And in the event that you are not a habitual magazine thumber, it would be well worth the time and expense it takes to buy a few current issues of magazines and study them from cover to cover. You might start with *House and Garden, The National Enquirer, Globe Midnight, Popular Science, TV Guide, The Mother Earth News,* and some of the big city Sunday Newspapers that have national distribution. Your eyes will be opened to a range of mail order offers you wouldn't have believed existed.

In addition to the thousands of firms that sell their products and services directly through magazine ads, there are many more doing business by mail who don't use magazine or newspaper advertising at all. Instead, they sell by "direct mail"; that is, by letters and circulars sent directly to prospects without benefit of prior advertising or solicitation.

Should you already be familiar with the tremendous scope of mail order, you may be slightly intimidated by it, and perhaps you are wondering whether, in a field that appears to be so crowded, there is room for *you.* The answer is an unequivocal "Yes." Instead of being discouraged by the great number of mail firms already active, you should take this as positive proof that mail order is a field in which many have found opportunity and profit...and there's always room for one more.

It may be a further source of encouragement to you to know that many of these firms, whose ads you see in magazine after magazine, year after year, are in reality small one- or two-woman operations. Some of them are operated as spare-time enterprises by people who hold down regular jobs. Others are "seasonal" operations, whose owners work like the devil filling orders during the heavy mail order season (roughly from September through April) and spend the rest of the year doing very much as they please.

If you are really serious about mail order, you can make yourself a place in this exciting business. You will soon have unearthed a product or two which look good for mail selling; and with a little luck and a lot of courage, you'll be buying ads, shipping orders, and banking the money, too.

If you are primarily interested in the profit potential of the mail order business, one of the first questions you will ask is "How much money can I make?" This is a proper question; even though as a businesswoman or man you must have a genuine desire to serve the public faithfully and well, you must also have a burning desire to make as much money as you honestly can. That, as they say, is what it's all about.

Answering the question "How much money can I make?" is a lot like answering the question "How high is up?" It all depends on your own vantage point, your own definition of what "a lot of money" is. To some folks, $50,000 a year may sound like a princely income. . .enough to support an average family in modest style. To others, nothing less than $1,000,000 a year is worth troubling themselves about.

In the mail order field, you will find both extremes. There are one-woman operations paying their owners $50,000 per year. There are part-time operations that supplement their operators' regular income, bringing in $15,000 to $20,000 a year. Then there a group of companies that net their owners as much as $5,000,000 per year and more.

There is no pat answer as to how much money you can make in the mail order business, any more than there would be as to how much you could make in the restaurant business or the computer selling business. It depends primarily on *you* and what you do with the abilities, facilities, and resources you have.

If you are now holding down a regular job and are looking to mail order to supply an opportunity for part-time employment and income, you could not have chosen a better field. For if you have a little capital to invest and a few hours each day to apply to the endeavor, you may eventually build a business that will release you from your job completely. There are few other forms of part-time activity that hold this promise. Mail order is perhaps the only field in which you can start a spare-time business on relatively little money, without interfering with your steady job.

How do you get started in mail order? Again, there is no precise answer. Everybody starts in a different way. But everyone who enters mail order for the first time usually follows a general pattern. First, you find a product or service which you think people will buy through the mail. Second, you decide where the largest number of logical prospects for this product are and which advertising medium (newspaper, magazine, direct mail) is best for reaching them. Third, you place an ad, or prepare a mailing, featuring your product or service. From that point on, the rest is persistence. You may make a new fortune from the first ad, or you may not get enough orders to pay for your postage. But in either case, this is the way you get started, and the outcome of this start is what usually determines the balance of your career.

It may have occurred to you that you rarely ever see a going mail order business advertised for sale. There are many reasons for this. One of them is that every mail order business is as individual as your bed, and is not adaptable to general use. Where one person can take an idea and make it produce wonders, another person might be a colossal flop trying to operate on the same idea.

Another reason you cannot buy a ready-made mail order business is that all those that are worth buying are so successful they are not for sale.

The best way to get started is to forget about buying a business which is already operating and concentrate on working up your own individual proposition. A good base from which to make this start is your own personality, interests, and tastes. For example, a women who was a department store saleslady is making a fine success of selling women's fashions accessories by mail. A woman who worked in a Vegetarian carry-out for years is doing extrememly well selling Vegetarian Cook Books by mail. A woman who was working in a Garden Nursery put her knowledge into a series of "how to garden" booklets and made a fortune. A fellow who preferred fishing to working finally quit his regular job after twenty years and started a mail order company selling a little gadget which he had devised on one of his fishing trips. To date he has sold a million dollars worth of these gadgets by mail and has made more money than he ever could have in his job.

You can easily see the moral in these illustrations. The best things to sell are the things you know best and like to handle best. The project you may now be pursuing as a hobby might hold the key to your mail order success. Or, perhaps, the work you are doing for a livelihood is the thing that interests you the most, and there is some aspect of that work that can be developed into a product or service which could in turn be sold by mail to others of similar interest.

Perhaps you have no special training, but nevertheless enjoy handling certain classes of goods, such as women's fashions, costume jewelry, or electronic games. There certainly is a world of mail order opportunity in all those lines. Before you make a haphazard selection of something to sell by mail, first make a survey of yourself and then select those things that suit your interests and personality.

It is important that you make your initial selection of a product as carefully as you know how—especially if you are operating on limited capital and cannot withstand a serious loss at the start. You will be inclined, and perhaps urged by others, to jump right in with a hasty, ill-considered offer.

Remember as you search for a product with which to start that there are thousands of good products around to sell and hundreds of manufacturers and wholesalers who are ready and willing to supply them to you at good discounts.

Remember, as in any other business, you cannot be successful with an endless parade of one-time customers. To make money, you have to sell these same customers, time after time, either more of the same product or related products.

Chapter 2

Mail Order Capital and Where To Get It

There is no hard-and-fast rule about how much money you need to start a mail order business. It all depends on the type of product you will be handling, what selling methods you will use, and how elaborate your facilities are to be. A good general rule of thumb, however, is to have enough money on hand to finance at least a two-month operation, whether you intend to start in the most modest way or on a much larger scale. And if you have a rich aunt who can lend you enough money to finance the business for five months, so much the better. Under no circumstances should you start with only enough money to operate for the first week. Not even the mail order business works well enough or fast enough to begin financing itself in so short a time.

Whatever else it is, mail order is also a gamble, despite the fact that you take every precaution to insure its success. Because putting money into mail order (or any other business venture, for that matter) is not unlike dabbling in the stock market you don't want to take any larger risk than is necessary. There are many ways you can reduce the amount of capital you need without instituting false economy measures.

You can, for instance, refrain from buying expensive office equipment and furnishings until you see whether your project is going over. Such things as filing cabinets, desks, and shelves can be improvised economically in the beginning from crates, boxes, and second-hand furniture.

You won't need a full-time secretary at the start; whatever correspondence is required can be done by part-time help or by your husband.

You will definitely need a good typewriter as you start your business, but you don't have to tie up precious capital in the purchase of a new one. You can either find a good used machine or rent one for a few dollars per month. Most office-supply firms will provide you with a typewriter on a rent-purchase agreement, under the terms of which you can apply your rental payments toward the purchase price of the machine if you decide you want to buy it later.

If you are on a regular job which pays you enough to take care of your living expenses and allows a surplus which you can divert into your business venture, you are in a fortunate position. In spite of the most careful planning, most new ventures require more capital than is anticipated, and you will be wise to begin thinking about where you can get additional amounts should you have a need for them.

The two largest slices of your available capital will usually be spent on 1) merchandise inventory; and 2) ads or direct-mail materials. You must have an adequate supply of stock to fill the expected orders from your first ad insertions or mailings. (This doesn't have to be a large inventory if you are in a position to get fast delivery from your supplier.) You don't want to keep your customers waiting for their orders; explaining why you haven't shipped the goods is more costly and time-consuming than shipping the goods.

The amount you'll need for ads or direct mail depends wholly on what you're selling and what type of magazine or mailing pieces will be used. In any case, it is good insurance to have enough money to carry you for the aforementioned two months. If you're using display ads, figure out what a month's advertising will cost; then set aside enough money to pay for it for two months. If you plan to sell by direct mail, figure out how many letters you can process and put into the mail per month and multiply by two

There are two admonitions which perhaps should be injected here in regard to direct-mail selling. One is that printing prices are terrifically high, and to keep your cost-per-letter down as low as possible, it is necessary to buy your printed materials in fairly large quantities. (10,000 to 25,000.) By planning a two-month mailing in advance, you can place orders with your printer for the total two-month quantity and receive the most favorable prices. The second admonition is that your printing must be of good quality; this is one area in which you cannot afford to skimp or try to get by with anything less than the best. Shoddy, cheap-looking printing will hurt your sales substantially.

In selecting a product or products to sell by mail, it is usually a good idea at the start to choose those in the intermediate price range—those which retail for $10 to $29. To sell an item that retails for less than $10, you have to pull a great many orders in order to make a profit over and above your costs. It takes a lot fewer orders at $10 per order to break even or make a profit than it does at $3 or $5 per order. Which brings us to a mail order truth that is worth remembering: It is usually easier to increase the amount of money received per order than it is to increase the number of orders received, all other factors being equal.

As you may already have guessed, the price of a product has a great deal to do with whether it will perform profitably by mail, and this is true without regard to the merits of the product itself, particularly in the case of a big-ticket item. If you examine a cross-section of mail order products now being sold successfully, you will see that a preponderance of them fall within the $10 to $29 range. This is not to say that relatively high-priced items cannot be sold by mail; as a matter of fact, many of them are, for prices ranging up to $200 and $400. *(The Sharper Image Catalog— 680 Davis Street, San Francisco, CA 94111— Is selling a Nautilus Abdominal Machine for $485, that, they say is going like hot-cakes on a Sunday morning in December.)* But in the beginning it is better and safer to stick with comparatively low-priced units in the range given.

Many profitable mail businesses have resulted from initial investments which now seem ridiculously low. On the other hand many millions of dollars have been wasted in attempts to start mail order businesses by big-time investors who erroneously believed that mere quantities of money were all that was needed to create a profitable mail business.

Most established mail order firms have beginnings which lie somewhere between these two extremes. Over three-quarters of the successful mail businesses now operating, according to a survey, were started with more than $5,000 in capital. About a third of them were begun with as little as

17

$1,000. There is not much consolation in having to begin on such a modest scale as $200 or $300, but there is this to consider: The less money you have to start with, the better businesswoman or man you will have to be; the better you will have to plan; the more wisely you will have to spend. Succeeding in spite of a lack of capital will—in later years—bring you as much satisfaction as you enjoy from scanning your latest profit statement.

The money you use to start a business-by-mail should not be borrowed money if you can avoid it. It should be money of your own to do with as you see fit, win or lose. Naturally, you don't want to deprive the kiddies of the necessities of life while you're getting your stake together.

The time you spend while you're waiting for your savings to grow to a sufficient level should be time devoted to study. Learn all you can before you start. Read mail order books; watch the offers in magazines and newspapers; talk, if you can, with other mail order people. You will also find it profitable and enlightening to pick out a few ads from the current publications; then check old issues of the same publications to see if identical ads were run in the earlier issues. (Most libraries contain back-number files of the more popular magazines.) If a product or service has been consistently advertised in a certain medium for a number of years, you can be certain that that product or service is a mail order winner.

If you propose to borrow money to finance your mail order venture, there are several loan sources you can consider. One is someone among your friends or relations who would consent to lend you the money without demanding an inordinate rate of interest and who would not be forever inflicting his or her advice on you. If you've got such a friend or relative, borrow as much as you think you need, and no more. Then work out a repayment arrangement that won't overburden your business during its crucial first few months.

The next best source for a loan is your bank. If you are an established resident of your community, your chances of floating an adequate loan are good—especially if you have assets or property that can serve as security. On the other hand, if you are not well known to your bank, and have not had previous loan experience with your banker, your chances are pretty slight. Bankers as a whole do not understand the mail order business and do not lend money on new ideas. Furthermore, banks hesitate to make speculative loans of any kind, except to big time entrepreneurs who have already proved that they know how to use money to make money.

Don't assume from this, however, that you might as well give up the idea of trying to get the money from a bank. By all means, go ahead and try; you never can tell when a banker will be in the mood to say "Yes." Before you call on him, though, work up a typewritten prospectus or outline describing exactly what you intend to do. This prospectus should clearly show what it is you plan to sell, how you plan to sell it, the amount of money you will need for starting inventory, the amount needed for ads or direct mail, and give a calculated guess as to the amount of profit you expect to realize from the effort. If you tell a convincing story and present a detailed, well-thought-out plan of action, you may get your loan on the spot.

Whether you need a loan in the beginning or not, it is not a bad idea to make a bank loan as soon as possible after your business begins to yield a profit. The purpose of this is to lay the groundwork for larger loans you may wish to make in the future when you need to expand your operations. As you know, each succeeding time you borrow money from a bank and pay it back as agreed, you build a continually increasing line of bank credit that will be indispensable later on. For instance, one young lady who started in the mail business went to her bank and borrowed $500 which she didn't need. She paid this back and shortly afterward borrowed $1,000. After about one year of additional borrowing and paying back money which she didn't need, this operator went to her bank and landed a $50,000 loan...which she did need. This, of course, was her objective all along, and it is through such foresight that small enterprises get to be big ones.

Chapter 3

How to Choose The Right Products to Sell By Mail

Some years ago a mail order specialist gained a certain amount of fame by making the statement, "Anything that can be sold can be sold by mail."

To inexperienced persons this can be a dangerous generality. It is undoubtedly true that there are a few rare mail operators who are capable of selling virtually anything by mail—and doing it at a profit. But the average mail order woman doesn't try it, nor does she need to.

To make it easy to enter mail selling without undue risk, there are a certain few categories of goods and services that come close to being ideal mail sellers; and, indeed, some of them could not be sold profitably any other way.

Before outlining these groups of sure-fire sellers, perhaps it would be in order to reiterate what was said a couple of chapters back about selecting a product. That is, the best thing for you to handle is something you like to handle. If you are a bookworm, you will probably be miserable attempting to sell sporting goods by mail. If you are an avid sportsman, you will rebel at the idea of selling books.

Generally speaking, you are most likely to be successful selling something which you create or make yourself, particularly if it has some originality or unique features about it. Similarly, your chances are enhanced when you sell something that is indigenous to your particular locale or region. For example, a Oregon firm does a substantial business selling *pears* by mail. In Oregon, pears are so abundant they alost give them away, but in eastern areas of the country, where pears aren't grown, people buy them readily.

A Florida woman does exceptionally well with *frozen sea food,* which is indigenous to her area. Nearly every part of the United States has some natural or manufactured product that is peculiar to it, and bringing such products to the mail-buying market at large can be very profitable.

If you are a talented person, you may be able to devise a mail order product or service based on your talent. For instance, if you are a health-nut, you can easily work up one or a series of instruction booklets on how to lose weight. These would be even more salable if you could think out and explain short-cuts to losing weight. There is a great demand for information of this kind.

If you like to work with your hands, you can turn out a course on how to make money with crafts. There must be a million people trying to make money selling their home made pottery, etc. and most of them are receptive to any information that will help them.

If you are a writer who has made money with an unusual business, you can put your knowledge, ideas, and business experience, into brief how-to manuals and sell them to aspiring "extra income opportunity seekers" through ads in *The National Enquirer, Globe-Midnight, Money Making Opportunities, etc.* There are any number of individuals doing this, some of whom are earning very respectable incomes.

If you are a housewife, you can turn this vocation into finding unusual gadgets for the home, office, or car. Millions of consumers buy gadgets of all kinds, from stick-on wall clocks, $5.95; to home tanning-sunbed systems at $3,995. If you could find an unusual gadget, you might be able to find a good market for it by mail. In this regard, don't attempt to sell a gadget that requires too much processing. Because if yur orders suddenly multiplied tenfold, you'd have a difficult time getting the manufacturer to produce enough of the articles quickly to fill the demand.

In this discussion about products which you should handle by mail, it has been considered that you might already have a pet idea that you'd like to try by mail. If you have such a pet idea or project, by all means give it some serious thought, without paying too much attention to how silly it may sound to you. Some of the greatest mail order ideas have, in the beginning, seemed downright absurd, yet later turned into astounding successes. Don't let friends, relatives, or neighbors influence you. Their judgement in this matter is not likely to be worth much.

If you have an original idea, don't submit it to your next door neighbor, or your best friend for appraisal. Instead, locate a responsible mail order sales counselor and tell him or her about it. He'll give you a reliable picture of its possibilities and tell you how to go about getting it on the market. Mail order counselors (the good ones) will charge you a fair price for their advice; but as you will discover, it is usually worth much more than what you pay for it. *(Direct Marketing Magazine lists several to choose from.)*

If you don't already have something in mind to sell by mail, you'll have an interesting time unearthing a product that you can purchase at a reasonable cost. A good start is to determine the general class of items which you want to handle (such as household goods), then subscribe to the trade journals which serves that field. These trade journals are real gold mines for the mail order operator, inasmuch as they contain announcements of new products as well as ads featuring all manner of items that can often be purchased directly from the manufacturer.

To illustrate the procedure for making a product search, let's suppose you decide that you want to specialize in household items. How do you find out who makes household items *cheap* and where to buy them? You could, of course, hop over to Hong Kong's biggest wholesale general merchandise store, if you lived in Hong Kong, look over the many items available, and arrange to buy them at big discounts. But if you don't live in Hong Kong, and you have no idea of how to get in contact with a wholesaler in that country, the thing for you to do is to find out what trade journal serves the household field. (There *is* such a journal, and it is called *Hong Kong Enterprise.*) In the pages of the trade journal, as I said, you will find every conceivable kind of household item and gadgets advertised by its manufacturer, distributor, or importer. Your job will be to select the item or items you want to offer by mail, get in touch with the manufacturer or other source, and arrange for shipment.

The above method of uncovering a mail order product, or a series of products, applies to nearly all classes of goods in all fields of business. It is not the only method, but it is a simple, effective one. It requires a bit of patience, and sometimes a bit of sleuthing to get your hands on the right trade journals and manufacturers' catalogs—since in some cases these are strictly "inside dope" and are not to be meant to be read or seen by anyone outside of the field.

In selecting your line of products, keep in mind that there are certain rules to which the items must conform to be good mail sellers. In the first place—and this is very, very important—the thing you sell must have a long profit margin. By "long" I mean anything from fifty percent on up. (Sometimes even fifty percent is not enough.) Trying to sell on too low a profit margin can mean losses or failure of an otherwise good mail order offer. It is one of the common errors which you should avoid. You can see that a retail store can get along nicely with thirty-to-forty percent profit because it has a large variety of products and a relatively low selling cost per item.

Hong Kong Enterprise
Hong Kong Trade Development Council
Great Eagle Centre, 31st Floor
23 Harbour Road
Hong Kong

U.S. OFFICES
333 North Michigan Avenue Suite 2028
Chicago, Ill. 60601
(312) 726-4515

548 Fifth Avenue, 6th Floor
New York, New York 10036
(212) 730-0777

350 S. Figueroa Street, Suite 520
Los Angeles, CA 90071
(213) 622-3194

But in mail order you have the additional expense of advertising and direct-mail materials. The cost of these has to come out of your gross profit. If your profit margin is too low, you won't have anything left for yourself after you've paid all the other costs. The fact that you have to have a big profit doesn't mean, of course, that your customer is paying more than he should for the product. There are many items available which you can buy for less than one-third of their retail selling price, yet which nevertheless represent good buys for your customer.

Besides allowing you a good profit margin, the product you handle must have something out of the ordinary about it. It cannot be something that is sold in shops and stores to any considerable degree. If you look over a group of ads in any popular magazine that features mail order advertising, you will notice that in nearly every case the product advertised is one that is not available in stores. And it will have something unusual or unique about it to distinguish it from similar products.

If you have an analytical turn of mind, you may find it both interesting and instructive to study a hundred or so current ads in mail order publications and classify those hundred products or offers. Without actually performing this analysis, you can take my word for it that nearly every mail order proposition will fall into one of the following classifications:

1. *Information*—This comprises correspondence courses, books, manuals, home study courses, newsletters pamphlets, etc. Most of these will have an instructional purpose: to show you how to do something, make something, or learn something. In the "information" phase of mail order, you'll find offers on a vast variety of subjects.

2. *Merchandise*—In this class will appear the gadgets, gizmos, gimmicks, and widgets. Things for the home, office, car. The range of merchandise sold is very great, extending from fancy foods to marine products to vitamins to stereo equipment. A million and one different products make up the "merchandise" phase of mail order.

3. *Personal Services*—In this class fall those specialized personal services by individuals or corporations who use the mails to promote their businesses or franchises.

If you choose to sell merchandise, you don't have to have a startling new invention to be successful. Choose a product that is already being manufactured by someone else and start selling it. If it goes over, pick out something else in the same general class and offer it, too. If you sold ladies' fashions, for example, you could logically add ladies' accessories which you'd sell to the same people who bought the women's apparel.

Follow this pattern long enough, and you will eventually have a whole line of products which will then lend itself to being developed into your own catalog. In selling by mail, and especially in selling tangible merchandise which you buy from others, you won't make a tremendous amount of money selling just *one* item. To build a volume of business, and thus a sizable profit, you have to sell different things—a *line* of goods. And once you've developed a large enough line, you can profitably switch from selling direct-from-ads or direct mail to catalog selling.

Perhaps the biggest single money-maker of mail order is the information selling field. The reason for this is not only that it is probably the safest and most profitable branch of the business, but also that it is the easiest to get into.

Information-selling requires little capital at the start and in general yields a higher profit return than any other form of selling, for the amount of money invested. Most items in the information field are just so much printed paper, and the cost of the product itself may be as little as five percent of the selling price. It's the information that counts, and for which your customer pays—not the quantity of paper or number of words.

The market for various kinds of information is really vast, and helping to supply the demand is not only financially rewarding but a good way to render a valuable service as well. Thousands of people are thirsty for knowledge on hundreds of subjects. They want to know how-to-get-rich, how-to-win-friends, how-to-lose-weight, how-to-use-computers, how-to-play-better-tennis, and so on.

If you can give them the knowledge or information they want, you'll be well paid for the effort. You don't, of course, have to open a big correspondence school or go into the book publishing business. Your information offering might be as simple as a twenty-five page booklet telling how to save time doing housework, or a ten-page newsletter on how to make money running garage sales or doing any one of a hundred different things. The information you sell can be as simple or elaborate as you want to make it. There is a demand, and a waiting market, for all kinds.

The best way to break into the information-selling field is to write up your own material and have it printed at a local printer. You don't have to have any pronounced literary ability. Just decide on a subject that you know pretty well, piece out your own knowledge by studying other books and courses on the subject, then write it up in clear, understandable language. Once written, the information is ready for publication. The method of reproduction is not too important as long as the finished product is attractive and easy to read.

The information field is perhaps the easiest one in which to build a line of related items. A person who buys one manual or booklet from you will buy additional ones on similar subjects if you have them to offer and if he or she was satisfied with his first purchase. With very little capital outlay, you can easily work up a series of small informational publications from which you stand a good chance of realizing an excellent income.

The number of subjects you can treat in this way is almost without limit. However, there are some general classes of information which sell better than others. The first of these is information on how to make money. Everybody wants to make money, and if you know of a way to do it, write your idea down and offer it through the mail. The most successful information sellers, as you can see by the ads, are selling information either directly or indirectly concerned with making money—in a thousand different ways.

Information on the various weight loss methods also sells well by mail. There now are—and always will be—plenty of people around who want to buy instruction manuals, books, and courses on how to repair automobiles, how to fix TV sets, how to build their own furniture, how to take better pictures, and similar subjects. If you or your husband have had sufficient personal experience in any one of the various trades, you might well work up a manual or booklet on the subject and offer it by mail. Don't let the fact that the same information is being offered by others stop you. In information selling there is always room for one more. This is particularly true of capsule courses of instruction, written to sell for a comparatively low price. For example, there are several high-priced courses on the market on the subject of real estate investing. These courses sell for $300 and up. Not everyone is able to pay so much for a course about real estate investing, so the way was clear for the development of a course to fill the lower-price gap. Along came a mail order firm with that very idea, and it is going over in a big way.

Money-making, health, beauty, weight-loss and sex are the big leaders in the information-selling field. But there are many other subjects which sell well and offer opportunity to newcomers. The writing-instruction field, as previously mentioned, is always open for a new approach to the subject of writing-for-pay. Everybody at one time or another decides she or he is destined to write the "great American novel." The majority of these would-be writers never get beyond the doodling stage, but they continue to buy great quantities of booklets, books, manuals, courses, and what you have on how to write.

Other subjects that are grist for the mail order mill are how to start and run a small retail store, how to vacation in California on $25 a day, how to learn low cholesterol cooking, how to operate a home computer, how to become a public speaker, how to get into politics, how to get a Government job, how to operate a collection agency, how to learn or do anything that will raise an individual's status and/or increase his income.

How to obtain books from discount book wholesale publishers instead of writing and publishing your own. Con-

ventional books sell by mail for the same reason that self-written manuals and courses sell. There are several advantages to selling books, not the least of which is that there are a vast number of titles to choose from, the product does not deteriorate, and you can usually set up a drop-ship arrangement whereby the publisher ships the books directly to your customer under your label. Another feature of handling books is the low postage rates which they enjoy. Ounce for ounce, a book travels cheaper than any other kind of product.

In selecting a line of books to offer, you will want to study the wholesale publisher's catalogs at length, selecting only those books that deal with money-making, self-help, and how-to-do-it topics. Most publishers will have several titles of this kind in their catalogs, and it is not too difficult to get yourself established as a mail order book dealer.

The best one I know is:

Outlet Book Company, inc.
One Park Avenue
New York, New York 10016

As stated previously, if you have a knack for making various objects in your home, you may find your mail order fortune there. This is especially true if you have designed or created a gadget which is distinctive for its originality or uniqueness.

Having such an original product provides you with exclusive control over the manufacture and distribution of it, and this exclusiveness is one of the great mail order success secrets.

If you don't have a idea, but nevertheless you or your husband are handy with tools, give some thought to making and selling handicraft items of a more staple variety. Such things as gun racks, Lazy Susans, door nameplates, tie racks, lawn furniture, and toys often turn out to be good mail sellers. Sometimes you can even sell the patterns for making such items, for a good price, to people who have workshops and are looking for unusual things to make.

Aside from the handicraft line, there is one other big field of merchandise which lends itself to small-scale manufacturing and selling by mail. This is the "Fast-Moving" Cosmetic Beauty specialty field.

If you want to go into the "Beauty Cosmetic Field", first study a few of the obviously successful mail order offers in the beauty line. A cursory examination of a group of women's magazines and National Enquirer type newspapers reveals several beauty products that appear to be meeting with mail success. Some of them are: "How To Look Ten Years Younger!", "How To Have That Movie-Star Look With Jojoba Oil!", "How To Hide Your Wrinkles With Aloe Vera," and so on. There is nothing to getting into the Beauty business after you've made a few contacts. You first decide on one of the products in the group which appeals to you most (perfumes, diet aids, facial massages, creams, lotions etc.), then you get in touch with one of the private label laboratories, and pay them to supply you with the product under your label. There are dozens of private label manufacturers that will produce these products with your label on them. They will supply the product, bottles, labels, and cartons. After you have inventoried a fair amount, you start your ad campaign. If you become as lucky as one firm recently, you might run an $800 advertisement into a twelve-million-dollar business, practically overnight. It does happen often, you might be the next *Revlon*. But in the beginning however, you can build a steady volume of business if you choose the right product and put forth the right kind of mail order sales effort.

Private Label Laboratories

Ambix Laboratories
210 Orchard St.
E. Rutherford, NJ 07037

Alba Chemical, Inc.
285 Country Road
Tenafly, NJ 07670

Aerosol Laboratories
5485 Ramsay Road
St. Hubert, Canada J3Y5S8

Akm Distributing
P.O. Box 20762
Dallas, Texas 75220

C & T Research Laboratories
29 Royal Drive
Forest Park, GA 30050

Classique Perfumes, Inc
10-02 44th Drive
Long Island City, NY 11101

Clay Park Labs
3339 Park Avenue
Bronx, NY 10456

Complete Cosmetic Service, Inc.
708 Third Avenue
New York, NY 10017

Consolidated Royal Chemical Corp.
1450 N. Dayton Street
Chicago, Ill. 60622

Custom Cosmetics Co.
736 Parkside Avenue
Brooklyn, NY 11226

Dante Inc.
40-15 Junction Blvd.
Corona, NY 11368

Fragrance Development Corp.
20245 Sunburst Street
Chatsworth, CA 91311

Lander Company
1530 Palisade Ave.
Fort Lee, NJ 07024

MK Laboratories, Inc.
424 Grasmere Ave.
Fairfield, Ct 06430

Vi-Jon laboratories, Inc.
6300 Etzel Ave.
St. Louis, MO 63133

Contemporary Cosmetic Group
75 Main Avenue
Elmwood Park, NJ 07407

DEP Corportation
12821 West Jefferson Blvd.
Los Angeles, CA 90066

Dynavest Company
P.O. Box 3749
Batesville, AR 72501

Goodier Corp.
400 N. Bishop St.
Dallas, Texas 75208

Life Labortories, Inc.
P.O. Box 9080
Van Nuys, CA 91750

Michaels, Fredda, Inc.
P.O. Box 6121
Providence, RI 02940

Weeks & Leo Co. Inc.
P.O. Box 3570
Des Moines, IA 50322

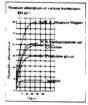
A.3 Private label companies can help you form your own line of cosmetics.

C.3 Diet Ads are the quickest way to a sizeable yearly income.

Chapter 4

How to Find Products To Sell

Finding one or more products to sell by mail can be as tough or as easy as you want to make it. If you close your mind, isolate yourself from the currents of trade information, and stand oblivious to the multitude of opportunities that constantly present themselves, you may well become a member of the chorus of mail order beginners who chant woefully, "But I can't find anything to sell by mail."

If, on the other hand, you are made of livelier stuff, you'll set your inquiring mind to solving the problem of something to sell, and will find more tempting opportunities than you will ever have time to try.

There are two general approaches to the problem of locating something to sell. One, you can determine the exact kind or type of product which you would like to handle, then go in search of someone to supply it. Or, two, you can go to a number of sources of supply without anything particular in mind, and from the variety of items thus examined, choose one or more of them to sell. One method is just about as effective as the other at the start.

Nearly everything manufactured in the United States for consumer use depends for its major outlets on the traditional retail store. (Although mail order is a "big" business, it represents only a small part of the total volume of goods sold through retail stores.) To get the goods to stores efficiently and quickly, most manufacturers work through wholesalers. In general, the wholesaler buys the goods from the manufacturer for about forty percent of the final selling price. He in turn sells the goods to the retailer for about fifty percent of the final retail price. (In sale parlance, retail price is often called "list price," and the wholesale price is known as "net price."

Now in the case of name-brand products, such as major appliances, certain brands of wrist watches, and so on, the wholesaler is often required by the manufacturer to limit the sale of these name-brand goods to specific "franchised" dealers. In such instances, the name-brand items are not usually available to mail order dealers, and it is largely a waste of time to try to handle such franchised products.

A wholesaler is within his rights to refuse to sell you certain classes of goods, because he owes it to his franchised dealers to protect them from as much competition as possible. Otherwise their dealership wouldn't be worth much.

Fortunately, though, most of the things that make good mail sellers are not franchised products but are items that a wholesaler will usually be glad to sell to any dealer who proves he is buying for resale and not for his own use. This includes mail order dealers.

Nowadays, there is more of a trend among manufacturers of specialty goods to sell their dealers direct, without going through the wholesaler. When this occurs, the manufacturer will in most cases sell to you at a somewhat higher discount than you normally would get from a wholesaler. There is no way of knowing which manufacturers will sell you direct, but it won't take you long to find out once you begin making inquiries.

Getting in touch with manufacturers is no problem if your town has a good library or Chamber of Commerce. Both these institutions customarily have copies of huge manufacturers' directors listing every important manufacturer in the United States, showing what he makes and where he is located. One of these directories is *Thomas' Register of American Manufacturers;* another is *McRae's Blue Book.* Both are extremely accurate and useful. Looking through these directories can be a revelation if you are not acquainted with the vast range and scope of manufacturing in the United States. And if you don't have any starting ideas for something to sell, a few hours spent thumbing through these books will give you plenty of ideas.

Should you find it inconvenient to have access to one of the directories mentioned above, the next best place to start on a product-search is in the telephone book. If you live in a small town, visit or write the nearest large city, asking for a copy of the phone book. In its yellow pages you will find listed all kinds of wholesalers and manufacturers offering all kinds of products. *(New York, Los Angeles and Chicago list the most.)*

In the yellow pages you'll find general merchandise distributors who offer a thousand and one items under one roof, and you'll find specialized wholesalers who offer a related line of specialty goods.

Whether you visit your wholesaler in person or get in touch with him through the mail is not important. However, if you're completely new to the business, you might find it works out better to make your first contact by correspondence, then follow that up later with a personal call.

As far as possible, it is a good idea for you to establish sources of supply close to home, regardless of what you choose to sell. Once you get your business moving and the orders are coming in at a rapid clip, it is vital that you be able to get new supplies as quickly as you can in order to keep the orders going out.

Of course, there are many products (particularly imported ones) for which there will be no close-to-home source of supply. In cases of this kind, the only thing you can do is lay in enough stock at one time to meet your anticipated volume of orders for a considerable length of time. Then, as your stock dwindles, enter another order well in advance, in time to have the additional goods before you run out.

Up to this point, you have a pretty good idea of what a product search entails, and you have been given the most expedient methods for making it. (There are others, such as attending trade shows, following "new product" items in newspapers like the *Wall Street Journal* and *Journal of Commerce,* and studying import bulletins.) You have a good picture of how goods get distributed, and the confidence that somewhere in this distribution system there is someone who can supply you with what you want. From this point on, it is mainly a matter of writing letters, asking for catalogs, and thumbing through brochures until you finally locate the products that appeal to you.

There are several things you should know, however, about writing letters to manufacturers, wholesalers, and importers to establish sources of supply. One of these—a definite must—is to use an attractive, businesslike letterhead. To do otherwise types you as a rank amateur and unworthy of the supplier's attention. So before you start corresponding with any potential supplier, get a printer to work up a letterhead for you showing your business name, address, phone number, and other pertinent information. It doesn't have to be a fancy job, but it should be neat, well laid out, and be on a quality paper with envelopes to match.

Another requisite of supplier correspondence is the use of a typewriter in writing your letters. Even if you have to hire a public secretary to type your letters for you, it is well worth the small expense involved. A handwritten letter gets little or no attention in the hard-bitten, fast-moving business world of today.

In corresponding with sources of supply, make your letters as clear and straightforward as possible. If you want their catalog, ask for it. If you want net prices on certain items, designate the names and numbers of the items in your letter. If you are placing an order, state the quantity wanted, the name of the item, the catalog number, and the price you expect to pay. As a rule, a good supplier is a pretty busy fellow, and he will appreciate your keeping your letters as short and to the point as possible, without leaving out any pertinent information.

One final caution in regard to corresponding with suppliers: If you are starting a new business, or if you are an established businesswoman but are new to this particular supplier, you will usually get better service and faster delivery by offering to pay for your initial purchases in advance. Don't send an order in in the expectation that it will be delivered on "open account" unless you have been advised by the supplier that he will ship to you on that basis. Before he can do this, he will want to make an extensive credit check, and this takes time. Too, by paying cash in advance, you frequently can earn small extra cash discounts that add to your profit.

Trade Shows

"McCormick Place" is the Nation's Market Place for trade shows. The address is: McCormick Place, 2301 South Lake Shore Drive, Chicago, Illinois 60616. If you don't do anything else you should attend the show of your choice. The cost of one weekend at McCormick Place is worth far more than the cost. (Book Hotels thru associations.)

The following is a list of Associations that put on a show each and every year at McCormick Place. You will find practically every Manufacturer and Importer represented there. Write them for future dates.

National Housewares Manufacturers
1324 Merchandise Mart.
Chicago, Ill. 60654

Chicago Gift Show
Eastern Manufacturers
261 Madison Avenue
New York, NY 10016

National Shoe Fair
230 W. 55th Street
New York, NY 10019

Chicago Computer Showcase Expo
300 First Avenue
Needah, Mass 02194

Consumer Electronics Show
303 E. Wacker Drive
Chicago, Ill. 60601

NOPA—National Office Products Show
301 N. Fairfax Street
Alexandria, VA 22314

There are many more shows at McCormick Place, too many to list. If you would like a schedule of shows for the next six months, send your request with a self-addressed envelope, include $.40 cents postage on it, to McCormick Place at the address listed above.

(The Consumer Electronics Show is my favorite, hope to see you there.)

Chapter 5

It's Not What You Sell It For, It's What You Pay For It That Counts!

You have probably heard it said that there is more profit in being a good buyer than in being a good seller. To a large extent this is true. By "buyer" I mean a person who can haggle and negotiate with a supplier until he has coaxed him out of another five percent discount. A jewelry retailer, for example, works on the assumption that there is a continuing market for his staple products. He knows, with almost absolute certainty, that eventually those twenty *Seiko* watches will disappear from his show case into his customer's hands. He doesn't have to force the sale of the watches (through promotion) because the market is already established, and if he waits long enough, someone will come in and buy one. But in mail order you have no such assurance; your first concern is always, "Will it sell?" and secondly, "How much can I buy it for?"

There are, naturally, certain fundamental purchasing practices that you observe in mail order just as in any other line of merchandising. One of these is to buy in the quantity which will earn you the greatest discount, commensurate with your capital. If the regular discount on *Product A* is forty percent in dozen lots, and you can get fifty percent off in lots of six dozen, then you will want to order the six dozen—provided you have a reasonable certainty that they will be sold within a reasonable length of time. And provided further that in ordering the larger quantity, you do not have to dip into the funds that are earmarked for other purposes, such as advertising and postage. If you're on short capital, you're better off to pass up the extra discount and conserve your cash.

Another good buying practice is to take advantage of the extra discount you can usually get by paying cash for your purchases. This will range anywhere from *one to five percent,* depending on your supplier, but the usual cash discount is two percent. This is over and above your regular dealer discount.

At this point, it might be well to interject a caution in buying for resale by mail. That is, to steer clear of "closeouts" or job-lots of merchandise which you can buy at a fraction of their original cost. Goods of this type often make a quick profit, but it's a one-time profit, and when they're all sold, you are out of business, unable to get any further supplies at a comparable cost. *(There are exceptions to this rule, and one is if you are going to specialize in just "closeouts." There are some companies that do very well in this field.)*

In the case of an item over which you have exclusive mail-selling rights (such as a product, or book you manufacture yourself), there usually arises the question of "How much will it sell for?"

The pricing of all goods is more or less arbitrary until they become so widely distributed that competition itself is the determining factor. In regard to standard consumer products, there is usually an attempt to relate the selling price to the actual cost of production and distribution, so as to yield a "reasonable profit." But in mail order, where you never know what your selling cost is going to be in advance, you meet with many occasions where you have to determine your own unit selling price.

In selling a standard product on which the retail price has been preset by the manufacturer, or has a more or less fixed value in the minds of the consumer, you would have to conform to this retail price should you offer the same product by mail. In such circumstances, all you can hope for is enough orders to cover your product, advertising, and incidental costs—and make you a small profit. Aside from aggressive promotion, there is very little you can do to put more profit into an item on which the selling price has already been established.

Where you are faced with the necessity of setting your own selling price on an exclusive product or offer, you will find a wider opportunity to build in some extra profit between the cost and selling price.

The "scientific" approach to arriving at a selling price is to *assume* that you are going to move, say, one thousand units per month—which in itself is very arbitrary thinking, but is at least a starting point. Now if you expect to sell one thousand of the items—let's call them Books—during one month, and they cost you fifty cents apiece (from the supplier, or printer), then your cost of goods or (books) is $500. (Put that down on a sheet of paper.)

Next, you *guess* what it is going to cost you in advertising space and/or direct mail literature and postage to pull one thousand orders. Suppose your guess is $1,250 for the ads and letters. (Jot down $1,250.)

You then figure out how much it is going to cost you to pack and ship one thousand books. Include in this figure the cost of one thousand boxes or cartons, the cost of labels, tape, postage, and whatever else you will need. Suppose you figure it will cost seventy-three cents each to put the Books in the mail. That's another $730. (Write that down under the other figures.)

From there, you estimate all the other costs of doing business during this representative month. Such things as *your* labor for a month ($250) and the labor of a part-time helper ($100) should be considered. With this, you throw in the rent and utilities (another $30), and anything else you can think of in the way of overhead. Oh, yes. Don't forget $25 for the rented typewriter. Altogether, this chunk of overhead adds up to $405.

Now comes the pleasant part. You decide how much net profit you think you are entitled to (over and above your labor) during the month in which you filled one thousand orders for Books and attended to all the other details of the business. How much did you say? $7,115? Well, that's fair enough. You earned it.

The next step is to add up all the numbers mentioned so far. If you wrote them down, it will be easy. If you didn't, here they are again: $500, $1,250, $730, $405, and $7,115. The grand total is $10,000.

Now all you have to do to find your selling price is to divide $10,000 by 1,000 Books. And doing so reveals that each Book should sell for $10.00.

But now that we've arrived at a "scientific" selling price, somebody is sure to raise his hand and say, "Yeah, but how do we know for sure that $1,250 worth of ads will sell a thousand Books?"

And someone else will ask the equally embarrassing question, "But isn't $10.00 an awfully, low price for a mail order product?"

And from the back of the classroom we hear someone else saying, "I don't give a hoot if we did figure it 'scientifically'; the Book looks like a good $15.00 dollars worth...so why don't we sell it for that, instead of $10.00?"

To which any experienced mail order operator would answer, "Let's do!"

If you are looking for a good list of Book Manufacturers that will print books (102 pages, 5½ X 8½) for around $.50 cents each. Here are some that I have used in the past. To get the $.50 cent rate; in most cases you must print at least five thousand copies. (It all depends on page count, trim size and the quality of paper used.)

BookCrafters
140 Buchanan Street
Chelsea, Michigan 48118
313-475-9145

The Book Press
Putney Rd.
Battleboro, VT. 05301
212-832-8880

Multprint, Inc.
28 West 23rd Street
New York, NY 10010
212-924-1100

Port City Press, Inc.
1323 Greenwood Rd.
Baltimore, MD. 21208
301-486-3000

Copen Press, Inc.
100 Berriemont Street
Brooklyn,, NY 11208
212-235-4270

Delta Lithograph Co.
14731 Califa St.
Van Nuys, CA. 91411
213-873-4910

Chapter 6

Center Your Mail-Order Company Around A "Related Line" Of Products Or Books

Unless you have a great deal of money to risk, and some prior mail order experience to go along with it, your first venture into mail order work will center around a few carefully selected *closely related* products or books. Most beginners start with just one item, and rarely more than two.

Restricting yourself to one or two offers at the outset provides a safe way of breaking into mail order while conserving your capital and giving yourself a chance to learn the business as you go along.

You will be tempted to try several different products or ideas at once, in the belief that such a "scatter-shot" approach is sure to bring in at least one winner.

But the newcomer is strongly advised to resist the temptation to begin handling several different offers simultaneously at the start—for two very good reasons. First, it is better to thoroughly promote one good item than it is to spread yourself *and your money* too thin trying to promote several different items. One product well sold is worth half-a-dozen haphazardly sold. The second reason you should limit yourself at the start is that, as emphasized in an earlier chapter, it always takes more money than you think it does to start a mail order business; and even though you feel you have more capital than you need to push just one item by mail, it is better to let this item start showing a profit before diverting your extra funds into other offers.

You will, with some success at the start, soon pass through the one-item stage and ultimately reach the point where you have a *line* of products or books, which in the aggregate produces a much larger volume of business (and profit) than can ever be done with one product.

You may have heard stories about mail order firms that rack up sizable profits year after year from the sale of only one item. There are such firms. But they are in the minority, and a newcomer would do well to enter the field with the understanding that although he is advised against trying to handle more than one item in the beginning, it eventually will take a line of products to build a really worthwhile business. In the interim, he will be working and learning and testing, and by the time he is ready to start building a line, he will have the requisite mail order know-how to do it successfully.

You may be wondering at this point how you go about selling a whole line of products by mail. (To do it entirely with expensive ad space would require an enormous advertising budget.) There are a variety of ways of going about it, but the most usual one is to offer a "leader," which can be the first product you started with. This may or may not make very much profit in itself. To the people who buy your leader from small display ads or classified ads, you send circulars describing other products similar in nature to the leader. Experience shows that if your customer was satisfied with his initial purchase, he will continue to buy additional offers to a very profitable degree. . .so profitable, as a rule, that you frequently can afford to sell the leader even at a loss in order to accumulate the customer names to which you will send the additional offers.

One mail order operator runs his line of offers in a manner analogous to a string of circus clowns. Each clown is led by the clown ahead of him and, in turn, is leading the clown behind him. In practice (and this works only where the products are very closely related in function or purpose), the use of each succeeding product depends on the buyer first having bought the offer ahead of it. Thus, the operator sells Item A, and shortly after he ships Item A, he sends literature describing Item B. As it happens, about twenty percent of the people who buy Item A also buy Item B. To the buyer of Item B, the operator sends literature describing Item C, and about twelve percent of the buyers of Items A and B also buy Item C. The process goes on indefinitely, until the operator has extracted every possible sale from his customers.

Other ways to merchandise a line of products are through a

catalog, periodic mailings of bulletins and flyers, or by stuffing your envelopes with groups of small circulars, each describing a different offer. One nationally known firm does it with postcards. But instead of sending out one postcard, it mails one long postcard which is folded and shrink wrapped around ten to fifteen smaller postcards to make a single mailing piece.

The catalog method is ultimately the most logical and most successful, but its main disadvantage is the high initial cost of preparation and printing. Nevertheless, it is the goal toward which nearly all mail order firms strive.

In building a line, there are several considerations you should take into account. One of these is that the additional items you add should be *similar in character* to your first or leading items, in order to make sure that your existing customers are good prospects for the additional items. Second, they should, so far as possible, be in the same general price range.

For example, if you succeed in selling a book on "How To Make Money" for $10, it is almost a sure bet that the person who buys it will be interested in buying a second book concerning money-making if it is priced in the same range. You wouldn't, obviously, turn around and try to sell the person who bought the money-making book a new kind of women's cosmetic or a revolutionary new resealable food storage bag. You would try to sell him or her more books related to the special interest she has already revealed by her first purchase.

Building a line, as in building any business, takes a great deal of time, thought and work. It is a fairly simple process, but it can't be done hastily. Most of the beginners who fall by the wayside do so because they don't have the stamina and patience to sweat it out for the first six or seven months. Either that or they try to expedite their growth by shoveling money into too many projects at once, and find themselves undercapitalized, undermanned, overworked, and underpaid.

Businesses of all kinds are long-term propositions, and they should be accepted as such. Mail order is no different. Relatively speaking, mail order often pays off quicker than any other type of business, but it takes a little time and effort.

The difference between reading of someone else getting rich in mail order and accomplishing it yourself is more a psychological one than a chronological one. When you read of a woman who made three million dollars in two years, your mind passes over those two years instantaneously, as though they were a mere snap of the fingers. But when you do it yourself, those two years can seem like a lifetime.

This is not to imply that you can't make such a sum in two years, or any other specified period of time. It has been done, and it will be done again. It all depends on who you are, what you are, and how hard you work, and other factors to arbitrarily set a certain period of time in which you will progress from a humble beginning to a millionaire.

Chapter 7

The Three Methods Of Mail Order

In mail order there are three general techniques for making the sale. All other methods are variations or combinations of these three established methods. They are 1) direct-from-ad; 2) inquiry follow-up; and 3) direct mail.

Method One is the one with which you are probably most familiar. It is simplicity itself. You insert an ad, either a display or classified, and use this ad to pull orders directly. Such an ad will tell your sales story in brief terms, quote the price, and ask for the order. You can find innumerable examples of this type of direct-from-ad selling just by glancing through any one of dozens of men's or women's magazines and nationally distributed (grocery store) newspapers.

Selling directly from the ad has several things to recommend it, but it also has several disadvantages and some severe limitations. The first of its advantages is the one which lures most beginners to this method of mail selling. That is, since the ad does all the selling, you are not bothered with the expense and labor in handling a lot of literature, circulars, envelopes, and the like. Furthermore, this method is immediate. There is no delay once the ad has been published. Each letter that comes in to you is sure to contain an order.

To employ the direct-from-ad method, about all you have to do is find a product, prepare an ad illustrating and describing it, then send the ad to the magazine or newspaper you have selected as the best medium. When the ad comes out, you will begin to get orders almost immediately, and they will continue for weeks, or possibly months. Sometimes an ad fails to produce a single order. Other times it will generate a young flood of orders. *(Good copywriting and informative illustration is the key.)*

For example, one firm has found that to sell its product—a gadget for the housewife—directly from the ad requires

$1,000 in advertising for each $2,000 worth of gadgets sold. In other words, $1,000 worth of display ads can be counted on to pull $2,000 worth of gross sales.

But on the other hand, this firm discovered after some testing that by running $200 ads (instead of $1,000 ones) which asked for inquiries only (instead of orders), and following up the inquiries with about $.8 cents worth of printed literature, it did more business. In the first instance, it cost $1,000 to sell $2,000 worth of gadgets. In the second instance, they had more housewives to mail their second offer to, and consequently made more sales.

My purpose here is to point out the merits and disadvantages of each of the three main methods of selling by mail—not to lay down any absolute rules about which is the "best," the "most profitable," and so forth. As I will attempt to convey here, and as you will learn as you get into the business, each product demands its own particular method. There are some products that sell best by direct mail, some that sell best by inquiry follow-up, some that can be sold most profitably directly from the ad.

In general, an item that is to be sold directly from the ad must be especially distinctive or unique in character, must be priced in the $10 to $19.95 range, and must be more or less an item over which you have exclusive control. In addition, it must carry a long profit margin (out of which you pay your ad costs), should be easy and inexpensive to ship, and should not be subject to appreciable breakage or deterioration.

An important point to remember when selling directly from ads is that the higher the price of the item, the more space you must use to get a profitable number of orders. An item that sells for $5, for instance, may produce a nice volume of orders from a Three- or four-inch display ad. But an item that sells for $10 would probably require a full page advertisement. And an item in the $39 to $49 range usually requires as much as two pages of display space. As the price goes up, so does the space necessary to sell the item.

Another consideration is that display ads (all ads for that matter) are seriously affected by seasons, much more so than the other two general sales methods. In general, a mail order display ad should be run in January, February, March,

August, September, October, and November. The other months of the year may produce as little as 70 percent of what was received in January.

There are many classes of goods which lend themselves to direct-from-ad selling: inexpensive gifts, self-improvement books, vitamins, diets, and hundreds of others. Some notable direct-from-ad sellers have been money-making books, new diets, small tools, cook books, watches, exercise equipment, and all kinds of consumer electronic products.

Method Two, making sales by inquiry follow-up, is as widely used as making sales directly from the ad, and for just as extensive a variety of products. It is a simple method, and an extremely effective one if you have a worthy product and the right kind of sales literature to follow up with. Briefly, the *modus operandi* is to place a small ad, either classified or display (some firms use both simultaneously), giving just the main points of your offer in their most appealing form and asking the reader to send you a card or letter for complete information. On receipt of her request for more information, you send her the prepared literature, then wait for her order. If you don't receive her order from the first follow-up within a reasonable length of time, you can, as some firms do, send her another follow-up letter, this time with more urgency in it, and perhaps offering an extra incentive, such as a discount or a premium, for placing her order at once. Depending on the nature of your offer and the price tag it carries, you can keep following up an inquiry indefinitely until you have exhausted every possibility of making the sale. Some firms will send as many as five to ten different letters to an inquirer, but such firms usually are selling products which carry relatively high prices—in the $100 to $400 range.

The real essence of a good inquiry follow-up is powerful sales literature. It is no trick at all to get inquiries if your offer is the kind that appeals to a fairly large group of people. A small investment in small ads will bring inquiries in by the sackful. They're worthless, of course, unless your follow-up literature is strong enough to convert a profitable percentage of them into sales.

The principal feature of the follow-up method of selling by mail is to eliminate waste—waste in advertising and in sales

51

literature. This waste normally is occasioned by the fact that in any given magazine audience there is usually only a small percentage of readers who are actual prospects for your offer. For example, a magazine may have a total circulation of five million copies, but out of that number of readers possibly fewer than a two-hundred thousand are actively interested in the thing that you are selling. To use a lot of display ad space to tell a complete story in such a magazine would be to address your message to 4,800,000 people who are not interested in your offer. This means that a large portion of your ad money has been wasted.

A far better way of reaching those among the readership who are prospects is to take the smallest size space that will accommodate the briefest possible message, and solicit inquiries only. By keeping such an inquiry ad going continuously, you will eventually reach virtually every prospect among the readership, at the lowest "per inquiry" cost.

The elements of a good follow-up are probably known to you already. If you have ever clipped out and mailed a coupon, or written a card or letter asking for more information about a product, you will recall that you got back an envelope containing these pieces: 1) a sales letter; 2) an illustrated circular; 3) an order form; and 4) a reply envelope. In addition, the letter may also have included a booklet, a premium coupon good for a discount or additional merchandise, a "testimonial" sheet, and possibly other items.

Now, if you want to operate a successful proposition by the inquiry follow-up method, your follow-up letter should contain all the above-numbered elements, plus whatever supplementary pieces you feel will help force the sale. These constitute the standard format for both inquiry follow-up and direct mail.

This is not the place to go into each of the various pieces in detail, but perhaps a brief description of each item's function would be in order at this point. The purpose of the first element, the sales letter, is to sell the prospect on the uses of the product concerned and dramatize the benefits it offers her. The letter tells her why she should buy the product, and buy it now—not later; it states the terms of purchase and the nature of the guarantee. It also clearly tells the prospect how to go about ordering the product: how much money she should send in advance and how to fill out the order form if it's unduly complicated.

The sales letter is not the place for, and rarely is used for, an actual physical description of the product itself. The letter deals only with uses, advantages, benefits, reasons why, terms, and guarantee. The description of the product is given on the circular. This is usually a printed piece, in one or more colors, illustrating the product, describing its physical features—dimensions, size, shape—and recapitulating the price, terms, and guarantee.

The other two elements, the order form and reply envelope, are self-explanatory. To get the most orders out of any given number of letters mailed, you must make it easy for your prospects to order. Bear in mind that not everyone keeps spare envelopes and stamps lying around the house, and a trip to town to pick up these things usually gives the prospect time to change her mind about ordering.

You must give your prospective customer an order form, for if she is required to write her order out on her own stationery, she often forgets to include her street address, the quantity she wants, or something else pertinent to the order. Also, the inclusion of an order form in your follow-up serves to encourage the prospect to buy today, rather than put it off until a later time. Remember that many people are lazy and that the simple acts of having to write out an order and find an envelope to mail it in are enough of a chore to cause them to put off ordering indefinitely. The easier you make it for them, the more orders you'll get. *(Don't forget the 800 toll free number. It sometimes can make a new offer when everything else has failed. But this, you'll have to test yourself on each and every new product you sell...... Keep in mind the 800 number is used on big ticket items, more often than on $10 items.)*

Nearly every good mail order product is adaptable to the inquiry follow-up method of selling, but some items lend themselves more readily to it than others. Products which are hard to describe in a few words, such as elaborate correspondence courses and electronic products, are best sold by this method. Products which are relatively high in price usually must be sold this way. On the other hand, items with a comparatively low price tag, i.e., $10 to $20, are most commonly sold by the direct-from-ad method.

The third general method of selling by mail is almost identical to the second, inquiry follow-up. The main difference is in the way names of prospects are acquired. In Method Three—direct mail—prospect names are gotten from sources other than publication advertising, and they are "cold" names, in the sense that these people have not taken the initiative in inquiring about your product or otherwise shown any active interest in it. The names you compile, rather than being "hot" interested prospects, are simply names of people whom you believe are logical prospects for what you are selling.

The sources from which you get these prospects' names and addresses are many and varied. There are mailing list houses who specialize in selling lists of names and addresses of persons who are likely to be prospects for nearly any class of products, books or services. These list houses can give you thousands or hundreds of thousands of names of people who have bought books, gifts, courses, household gadgets, diets and so on. Other sources for names are other firms who are active in mail order and who are willing to sell you a list of their own customers. The latter practice is widely engaged in—where the list users are noncompetitive—and can be extremely profitable for both parties. (A later chapter will deal with the development of a good prospect list in more detail.)

The direct-mail method of selling is exactly what its name implies. It is direct—from you to your prospect. No magazine ads in between. No cost of producing an inquiry. No time lost while waiting for an ad to come out. Selling by direct mail is simple in principle. You think you have a worthwhile product, book or service to offer. You think you know of a group of prospects who logically should be interested in buying it. So you sit down and write a letter to them and ask them to buy your product. That's direct mail—and anything else anybody says about it is just an elaboration of that simple formula.

Direct mail is one of the most astounding profit-making sales methods ever devised, provided you qualify it with a few ifs and buts. Few persons fully comprehend the power of direct mail to accumulate customers, and it may be just as well. The reason that more people don't fully understand it is that it literally has to be experienced to be understood. The source of that power is statistics and how to apply them to your mailings. You can operate successfully without a deep knowledge of statistics (or the "law of averages"), acquiring a working acquaintance as you go along, but any time you can devote to the subject of statistics and their application to the direct-mail business will be time well spent. (Direct Marketing Magazine and DM News publish monthly magazines and newspapers on this subject which are well worth studying.)

Ideally, the direct-mail method would embrace a good product that is in demand by the "right mail-order buyer list." The product would be one that measures up to all the standards of a successful mail order product, i.e., long profit margin, repeat potential, exclusivity, etc. *If* you had such a product, and *if* you had a direct mail solicitation that would pull a profitable number of orders, and *if* you could get a continuous supply of the "right" names and addresses to which to send the offer, then you could get rich in short order—that is, if you could get enough postage money together to finance a mass mailing.

For example, suppose you had an item which ten million people logically would buy. Suppose further that you succeeded in developing a sales letter and circular that were good enough to bring you $500 profit every time you mailed a thousand letters. Given this ideal set of circumstances, you would have made $500,000 by the time you had reached only one-tenth of your total market. By the time you had mailed to the entire list of ten million people, you would have made a profit of $5,000,000! And by the time you had mailed the offer to every person on the list just one time, it would have been time to start mailing the entire list again with a related offer. You would, in short, have what amounts to an infinite market, and with the law of averages guaranteeing your profit, the only thing between you and a fortune would be *time.* It does take a little time to process and mail ten million letters.

In practice, you can do very well indeed, if you are careful, even with a much smaller market, a reduced profit per thousand, and a much smaller mailing rate. It's being done all the time by firms who go along quietly year after year making big-money and creating steady customers by direct mail.

If you are brand new to mail order, you will do well to learn all you can about direct mail, but use it on a minor scale until you are sure you have enough capital to support a large, steady mailing campaign. For the beginner, direct mail is not as safe a bet as the direct-from-ad method or the inquiry follow-up method.

Direct Marketing	DM News
224 Seventh Street	10 West 21st Street
Garden City, NY 11530	New York, NY 10010

Chapter 8

How The "Pros" Do It

The preceding chapter describes the three general methods of making sales by mail. With an understanding of these methods, the following examples can show you how they are put into practice by different firms selling different products. In reading over these examples, pay particular attention to whether the product is sold directly from the ad, by inquiry follow-up, or by direct mail; and see if you can determine why each particular method is used.

The first example is a big one: Hume Financial Education Services. *120 Interstate N. Parkway E., Atlanta, GA 30339* This company sells: Successful Real Estate Investing. The cost of its course to the invester is $250 to $300. The method of selling is inquiry follow-up. Using display ads of many different sizes, in magazines and Newspapers ranging from *The Wall Street Journal, New York Times,* to *Inc. Magazine,* the inquiries thus received are followed up by elaborate mailings, which spare no effort to describe and sell the course to the prospective invester.

New Start Publications, a book publisher in Washington, D.C., sells a line of income opportunity books. These books are in the $10 to $12 range, for the most part. Each book is a complete course of instruction on such subects as: Close-Out Furniture Sales, promoting, mail order, and mind-improvement. Initial sales are made by the direct-from-ad method. Using full-page ads in mass publications such as *Popular Science Magazine, National Enquirer, Money Making Opportunities, Entrepreneur, Dallas Morning News, and The Los Angeles Times,* to name a few. Orders are pulled directly without benefit of follow-up. Each ad has a coupon in the advertisement. Each ad asks for money with order. After a person has become a customer, he then receives, four or five different follow-ups, ranging in price from $1 to $191 dollars.

A man in Illinois has for years successfully sold Vitamins using the direct-from-ad method exclusively. Mediums used vary widely, from the *The Star* to AAA motorist magazines. The ad is a full-page job, with order coupon, and asks directly for the cash order. Average cost of the vitamins is $5. As far as is known, no direct mail or inquiry follow-up is used in making sales. *Nutrition Headquarters, 104 W. Jackson, Carbondale, Ill. 62901*

A company in Georgia, *U.S. Optics, P.O. Box 14206, Atlanta, GA 30324,* sells sunglasses, which they buy in the Far East for $.50 cents to a dollar and sell for $9.95 to $14.95. They are sold directly from the ad. No inquiry follow-up or direct mail. Small display ads (about 2 inches by 6 inches in size) are used exclusively. The ad emphasizes the credit card purchase. Magazines used are: *Playboy, The Star, National Enquirer, Popular Science,* and others reaching a male consumer audience.

A mail order firm in Mount Vernon, NY, *Lillian Vernon, 510 S. Fulton Ave., Mount Vernon, NY 10550,* sells a line of gifts and specialty items in varying price ranges, but the average price is probably $10 per item. The firm uses direct-mail methods. The direct mail takes the form of a catalog mailed to names of buyers rented from mailing-list houses. The lists used are made up of mail order buyers of tableware, toys, leather goods, health and beauty aids, etc. *(They mail 35 million catalogs a year.)*

The Eddie Bauer Company of *15010 N.E. 36th Street, Redmond, WA 98052* sells a line of sporting goods, a few of which the company itself manufactures. The principal method of selling is to use a series of small display ads, each ad featuring a different product. These ads ask for the order directly, but also make the offer of a catalog. Products range in price from $40 to $125. Purchasers of items direct from the ad receive a catalog follow-up. Mediums used are the sporting and outdoor magazines, such as *Outdoor life, Field & Stream,* and *Sports Afield.*

There you have a few examples of well-established, nationally known mail order firms, what they sell, and the methods they use to sell it. These examples are given in brief form, but sufficient information is given to enable you to understand why a particular method is used for a particular product. The fact that all of these firms are reputed to be highly successful ones (some of them doing millions of dollars worth of business per year), and the fact that their success was won entirely by mail, proves that they wisely adapted the right mail selling method to their respective products.

Choosing the right method is another of the all-important "secrets" of mail selling. Many projects have failed through a lack of careful selection of the method to use. Some dealers try to sell directly from the ad, when they should be using direct mail. Others use direct mail when they could sell more profitably direct from the ad. Others could be profitably using all three methods, yet are limping along on just one.

I have tried to indicate and emphasize that each individual product or offer demands its own method, and that there is no pat formula for determining which is the best method to use, short of trial and error. Discovering the best method for *you* to use is partly a process of reason, based on factors previously outlined, partly a matter of experience, but largely a matter of *testing*. Test one method; then test another. Now test them together. Then revise the copy and test them again. Test them for the best seasons, the best ad mediums, the best sales-letter copy. Test the price, the terms, and the guarantee.

Newotics Optical Industry Co.
B3 Chi Hiong Mansion, 58-60 Camerin Rd.
Tsimshatsui, Koowloon, Hong Kong

Manufacturer/exporter of fashionable sunglasses.

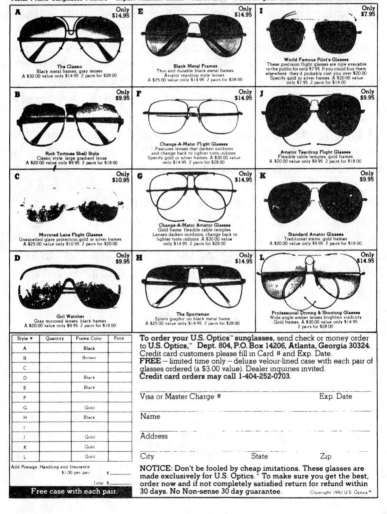

Chapter 9

The Advertising Game

If you have a product which you think will sell, but you don't want to attempt to sell it by direct mail or the inquiry follow-up method, there are three general ways in which to bring it to the attention of a great many prospective buyers.

These three ways, or media, are 1) magazines; 2) newspapers; and 3) radio and television.

Radio and TV as media to produce volume mail sales have been profitably exploited by several firms with the expert know-how required. Conversely, they have been tried by many firms that did not have the special knowledge or experience, and severe losses resulted. For the beginner's purposes I would rule them out altogether, unless the beginner has plenty of money to risk and plenty of mail selling experience to back it up—in which case she wouldn't be a beginner.

With radio and TV out of our way, we have only two media left to discuss. We'll consider these in the opposite order of their importance to the mail order aspirant. Newspapers as a mail order medium are, to a large degree, ineffective, expensive (reader for reader), and short lived. Any one of these reasons is enough to discourage the use of newspapers. However, there are a few exceptions. These are the big metropolitan papers that publish Sunday supplements, *Parade and Family Weekly* special out-of-town editions, and mail order sections. This group of papers is used consistently by many mail dealers with good results. Some of the papers so used are the *Chicago Tribune,* the *New York Times,* the *Los Angeles Times,* and the *Dallas Morning News.* A complete listing of them here would serve no constructive purpose. If you live in handy proximity to a well-stocked newsstand, you can find any number of them there. In fact, it might pay you to buy a few of them and study the Sunday mail order sections. You'll get some idea as to what is being sold and what may be sold via newspaper advertising.

Using full page advertisements in the major metropolitan papers has both advantages and disadvantages. One of the advantages is that an ad can be placed and published in a very short span of time. This is a considerable advantage when you are in a hurry to test a new ad or product. Whereas you frequently have to wait four weeks to two months for your ad to appear in a magazine, you can submit it to a newspaper one week and it will be in the readers' hands the next. Rarely does a newspaper require you to wait more than three days for your ad to appear.

A second advantage of using newspaper space for mail order is that it provides a good proving ground for new products and different ads at relatively low dollar outlay. Before splurging a large amount of money on ad space in a big national magazine, you can often test the offer with reliable accuracy in the newspapers. Naturally, the results you would get from such a test would be more indicative than conclusive, but they would tend to show weaknesses in the offer or ad copy, which could be corrected before placing more costly ads in magazines.

The products that will sell well from newspaper space are usually the same ones that will sell from magazine space. However, a preponderance of products sold through newspapers are utilitarian—items which have a practical use—such as gadgets for the kitchen. Another group of these offers is in: money making opportunity books and diet aids. There is one outstanding feature of any product that can be successfully sold through newspapers, and that is that it must definitely appeal to a mass audience, since newspaper audiences are not selective, screened, or specialized as is the usual case with a magazine readership.

The fact that an ad can be published in a newspaper without too much delay also means that newspapers are quickly prepared, and just as quickly read and thrown away. Even if you use one of the special weekly magazines like *Parade*, the life of the ad is much less than it would be in a monthly magazine. While a newspaper ad will pull for two or three weeks, a magazine ad will often pull for three months or more. The reason for this is simply that newspapers are discarded soon after they are read, whereas a magazine will lie around the house or office for months, and it frequently is read and reread by several people other than its owner.

A disadvantage of newspapers is that they do not offer an opportunity to do selective selling, as previously pointed out. They are edited and published for indiscriminate masses of people. If you tried to reach a specialized group of prospects—electronic store owners, for instance—through a newspaper ad, most of the circulation for which you paid would be wasted. The number of electronic store owners among any newspaper readership is mighty small, perhaps less than one-tenth of one percent. It would not be good advertising practice to pay for ten thousand unwanted readers in order to reach ten you did want. A far better procedure is to spend your ad money in the pages of a electronic trade journal, where every reader is a electronic store owner.

It is this quality of selectiveness, combined with widespread circulation, that makes magazines the best all-around mail order medium. For magazines—as opposed to newspapers— are edited for specific groups of people who have certain interests and characteristics in common.

Because magazines are aimed at specific groups of people, however large they may be, the magazines themselves can be classed in definite groups by their editorial characteristics. As a future mail order operator, it will pay you to learn these groups of magazines, in a general way, although nothing will be gained by your knowing the names of every magazine in every group.

Nearly all magazines suitable for mail order purposes can be classed in the following groups: general news magazines, farm magazines, women's magazines, men's magazines, hobby magazines, business magazines and trade journals. There are other groups, such as the "quality" magazines edited for intellectuals; "religious" magazines and papers edited for various religious organizations and denominations; and the scientific publications edited for scholars, scientists, and teachers. Inasmuch as these latter groups are not suitable for mail order advertising, there is little point in your giving them much study.

The general news magazines are edited and published for the family group in the middle-income bracket. If you could isolate and examine a typical subscriber to one of the news magazines, like *Time, or Newsweek,* you'd find he was married, had a wife and a couple of kids, owned his own home, earned somewhere around $35,000 per year, and was for the most part a pretty average guy. You'd find that the general news magazine to which he subscribes is so written and edited as to interest in some way every member of the family above diaper age. Some examples of the largest family magazines are *Time, Life,* and *Newsweek.* Curiously enough, while the news magazines are great *National* ad media for standard-brand products sold in stores, they usually perform very poorly for mail order offers, or their advertising rates are so high they preclude use by the average mail operator. If you study a current copy of any of the magazines mentioned, you will find only a few, if any, mail order offers in their pages, for the reasons mentioned.

Closely akin to the general news magazines are the adult consumer publications edited on a male and female basis, each catering to the interests of the respective sexes. These magazines, on the contrary, are usually very good mail order media, and are used extensively to sell a wide variety of mail order goods and services.

In the male group are such magazines as *Playboy, V.F.W Magazine, The Elks Magazine, The Family Handyman* and *American Legion Magazine.* In the female group are *Woman's Day, Modern Maturity, McCall's Needlework and Crafts, Glamour, Parents, Savvy* and others with a slant toward the modern woman.

Then there are the so-called shelter magazines, which comprise an excellent group for mail selling purposes, particulary items in the gift-and-gadget line, products for the home, garden, or workshop. Among these are the familiar *Better Homes & Gardens, Good Housekeeping,* and *Organic Gardening.* A study of the ads in the mail order section of any or all of these publications would be worth the time expended, because many of the advertisers shown are very successful and their techniques worth emulating.

The farm magazines, as a whole, are also very good mail order advertising media. The reason for this is obvious. Rural people are isolated, to some extent, from city life, and their principal contact with the urban world is through farm papers and magazines. It is in the advertising columns of rural publications that they are able to keep track of new products and services and find new things of interest to them.

Many mail order firms depend almost wholly on farm publications for their sales. Naturally, to use these publications profitably, you must have a product or service which fills a rural need. Among the items being successfully sold to this market are film-developing services, plants and bulbs, formula compounds, tool, cutlery, Bibles, seeds, and building plans. There are many magazines in this group, varying widely in editorial content and form, but some of the better-known ones are *Progressive Farmer, Capper's Farmer, Grit,* and *Farm Journal.*

In the vocational and hobby group (including the science and mechanics magazines), we have perhaps the most productive mail order media available for an extensive variety of products and services. These magazines are edited for people who want to learn how to do various things, who want to extend their range of practical knowledge, with or without the profit motive.

In this group are the so-called mechanics magazines, which show their readers how to construct things, how to repair things, and how to understand scientific and mechanical things. Whether for amusement, amazement, or profit, their readers want to learn. It is this group that is the most receptive to mail order offers related to their interests, and you have only to look at a specimen magazine for proof of this. Every conceivable kind of book, tool, gadget, of course instruction, and plan is being offered. Some of the leading publications in this group are *Popular Mechanics, Popular Science, Mechanix Illustrated, Science & Mechanics, Workbench,* and *Crafts and Hobbies.*

Similar to, and partially overlapping those listed above, are the hobby magazines, both special and general. There are specialized hobby magazines edited specifically for such fields as photography, model trains, and stamp collecting; and there are those aimed at the hobby field in general. These, like the mechanics magazines, are excellent mail order media for products that cater to their readers' interest.

The final group with which we are concerned is the trade journals. This group comprises a vast array of publications serving every business and professional group. Each of them is written and edited along the lines of interest of each particular business, trade, or profession. There are trade journals for barbers, trade journals for motel operators, trade journals for bankers, dentists, doctors, lawyers, druggists, florists, garage mechanics, bill collectors, architects, and operators of service stations and hundreds of others. These journals provide a tailor-made medium when you wish to sell a specialized product to a specific group of prospects. There are dozens of flourishing mail order concerns who operate no other way. To delineate all of them would take more space than we have here; it should be sufficient to say that as an aspiring mail order operator, it will be worth your time to learn more about the field of trade journals, as well as the other groups of mail order publications. The most expedient way to do this is to get hold of a recent copy of the Standard Rate & Data directory for "Business Publications." You should also have the SR&D directory for "Consumer Magazines," as well as their newspaper directory if you plan to use newspaper advertising. Copies of these famous directories may be purchased from the publisher, Standard Rate & Data Service, Inc., 3004 Glenview Rd., Wilmette, Illinois 60091. Or, if an advertising agency will be handling your ads, it will have these directories on hand for your use.

BIG CITY NEWSPAPERS AND SUNDAY MAGAZINES. This medium of advertising is very tricky, but I am listing a few here that have worked very well for me in the past. Go slow on these publications. Test and test again before rolling out a full run. Try to always run a full page ad and try to locate an advertising representative, listed in the front of the *Newspaper S.R.D.S. Directory,* that can sell you ROP space. ROP Space is where the newspaper places your ad, at their discretion, on any page, on any day they choose, within two weeks. The GOOD part is that running your ad ROP gives you a large discount; sometimes as much as 50 percent off.

FAMILY WEEKLY
641 Lexington Ave.
New York, NY 10022

WALL STREET JOURNAL
22 Cortlandt
New York, NY 10007

PARADE
750 Third Ave.
New York, NY 10017

NEW YORK TIMES
229 W. 43rd St.
New York, NY 10036

LOS ANGELES TIMES
Sunday Classified Section
Times Mirror Square
Los Angeles, CA. 90053

CHICAGO TRIBUNE
435 N. Michigan Ave.
Chicago, IL. 60611

SEATTLE TIMES
Fairview Ave. & John St.
Seattle, WA. 98111

The Detroit News
615 Lafayette Blvd.
Detroit, MI. 48231

ATLANTA JOURNAL
TV Guide Section
PO Box 4689
Atlanta, GA. 30302

SAN FRANCISCO CHRONICLE
Sunday Book Section
Back Cover Only
Sawyer Ferguson, Walker Co.
212-661-6262
New York, New York

DM NEWS

AUGUST 15, 1983

THE NEWSPAPER OF DIRECT MARKETING

A New Direct Mail Association Is Due To Be Born This Month

Approval Expe

NEW YORK—A n association devoted to t the mail order indust establishment by mor ecutives who are r "originators" of the o

DM News learned source that a steering has been working quie the concept will originators on Tues present ideas for the executive director didates, develop a c membership rules.

The name rental new organization & Suppliers A

bolted from membership due to a large increase in dues, the dropping of the ... from that association's ...ages."

THE REPORTER OF DIRECT MAIL ADVERTISING • The magazine of

Direct Marketing
A Monthly Forum Devoted to Business Communications in Selected Markets

AUGUST 1984 • $3.2

Folio:
MAY 1983
PART ONE OF TWO
$4.00
THE MAGAZINE FOR MAGAZINE MANAGEMENT

PUBLISHING MANAGEMENT
Inside the organizational frameworks of six very different publishing companies

Measuring your editorial health

How to save a failing magazine

PLUS:
Production:
Buying in a buyers' market
Circulation:
What is a good response?

PUBLISHER

A.9 Folio—125 Elm Street, New Canaan, Conn., 06840
DM News—19 West 21st Street, New York, NY 10010
Direct Marketing—224 7th Street, Garden City, NY
11530

Chapter 10

Without Magazines, You and I Would Be Out Of Luck

Many mail order firms depend almost wholly on magazine advertising to secure their orders and inquiries. Indeed, without magazines, a newcomer would be out of luck, because the use of them represents almost the only way a new firm can get started safely and on little capital. In the absence of magazine advertising, direct mail could be used to start a new venture, but as pointed out earlier, this method of selling is not the best one to use unless you have a good working knowledge of it beforehand.

Incidentally, much ado about nothing has been made over the terms "mail order" and "direct mail." Direct mail people are quick to claim that they are in the direct mail business, *not* the mail order business. Others claim that the only simple-pure mail order is the kind wherein the order is received directly from the ad, and that—in agreement with direct mailers—direct mail is something altogether different. If you like to indulge in such semantic hair-splitting, you can find plenty of conversation among others in the business. For all practical purposes, we can dismiss the subject forthwith by saying that mail order is an all-inclusive term comprising all the various methods of getting business through the mail, and that direct mail is a name for one of those various methods.

Magazine ads are of two main types: *display* ads and *classified* ads. A classified ad is set in straight type, with no illustrations or decorative matter, and appears in long columns with many other similar-appearing ads, all of which are classified according to various headings, such as "Business Opportunities" and "Help Wanted."

A display ad is, in effect, a miniature billboard. It can be, and usually is, dramatized with artwork, photographs, and eye-catching gimmicks of all kinds. The type matter itself may be specially selected to enhance the nature of your message. And, too, a display ad is more likely to be placed in a position in the magazine where it will get the greatest amount of reader attention.

Another distinction between classified and display ads is in the way you normally pay for the space used. In buying classifieds, you pay so much for each word in the ad. In buying display ads, you pay a certain rate per line or per inch. The display "line" does not mean a line of words. It is a unit of depth and has nothing to do with the number of words in the ad. In a column inch of display space (one column wide) there are fourteen lines. So the magazine you plan to advertise in says its rate is so much per line; you multiply this by fourteen to find out how much an inch of space will cost you.

There are many things to be said about magazine ads, not all of which will be said in this chapter. One of the generalities I can set forth, however, is that if you plan to sell an item directly from the ad (with no follow-up), you will need to use display space, except in rare instances. If, on the other hand, you are merely seeking a flow of inquiries which you intend to follow up with additional literature, you can usually get them with fairly small amounts of classified space.

About the most important thing we can say about magazine ads is that they must be repeated, *in different magazines,* if their full effect is to be felt. This is perhaps the hardest thing to get across to a novice advertiser. That few of them understand and appreciate the effect of repetition in advertising is evidenced by the great number of one-time advertisers in mail order who buy just one ad, in one magazine, in the hope that it will somehow produce a tremendous volume of orders, and then quietly disappear from the mail order scene.

Repetition in mail order advertising—as in any other advertising—is a powerful force for success, provided, of course, that the ad to be repeated is a good ad featuring a good product in a good magazine.

There is no hard-and-fast rule about how much the returns from an ad will build up (or "pile up") under the impetus of consistent repetition. This varies a great deal from one offer to another. *Crossover readership is the key.*

Each consecutive insertion in different, but similar magazines, continues to increase the build-up until the maximum pull is reached (which may be at the sixth or twenty-sixth insertion). Once the maximum pull is reached, repetition will keep it at that level until you have skimmed the cream and it is time to try something else. But even after you have withdrawn such an offer, don't throw it away. Keep it in the files; chances are good you can start it again in two or three years and find that it pulls as freshly and profitably as it did the first time around.

Example: The Joe Karbo income opportunity advertisement has been running since 1972, nonstop. Joe Karbo passed away a few years ago, but his wife still continuously runs the advertisement at a profit.

There are several good reasons why an ad works better the longer it runs. The build-up is due partly to the fact that the first time an ad appears, it is seen by comparatively few readers. (We're speaking of the typical small-space mail order ad, not the full page blockbuster.) Each time the ad is repeated, it is seen by an increasing number of readers. Another reason is that a lot of mail order buyers, as a matter of policy, do not answer an ad the first time it appears. They wait to see if it appears again next month. If it continues to appear in consecutive or periodic issues of similar magazines, then they assume it to be a legitimate offer by a reliable firm and take action.

Then there are many readers who see an ad that interests them and make a mental note to answer it "in a few days." But sure enough, they simply forget it, or the magazine becomes misplaced, or they find they don't have the money at that moment. But next month when they see the ad again, they sit down and send you an order.

An additional factor in the build-up of returns is that magazines are often collected by subscribers and saved indefinitely. Many homes have collections going back for years. These are occasionally referred to and reread, and the old ad gets another crack at making a sale. Most veteran mail order operators can cite instances in which they receive orders from ads published several years previously.

Because of the factors just described, a successful mail order ad in a mass-circulation magazine can be repeated indefinitely without changing the ad's copy, size or appearance. If you can find a complete collection of *Popular Mechanics, Popular Science, Mother Earth News,* or some of the other workhorses of mail order, you might check back and note how many different ads have been running for years without change.

There is one other important factor that makes constant repetition possible. This is the phenomenon of reader flux; that is, a steady change in the magazine's readership from month to month and year to year. One authority refers to this flux as a parade, in which you, as an advertiser, are constantly viewing a passing throng of people, but you never see the same group of paraders for very long at a time. To put it more understandably, perhaps a magazine is continuously adding new readers and dropping old ones. Therefore, each new issue is read by a somewhat different group of people. Some of last month's readers will have died; others will have cancelled their subscriptions; some will have moved away. In the meantime, new readers have entered their subscriptions and started buying on the newsstands, and you have these as brand new prospects.

It is true that the bulk of a magazine's readership remains fairly constant, but over a period of time it will reveal a definite pattern of turnover. No figures are available on how long it takes a readership to turn over, but possibly seven to ten years would be a good guess. The significance of this turnover is important to you, as a future mail order advertiser, because it makes it possible to run the same ad indefinitely without change. Thus, your ad never gets stale, never saturates the market, because the market is itself in a state of change, and the ad is always new to a new reader. For example, if a magazine has a circulation of 1,800,000 copies, *Popular Science* and its turnover period is seven years, this means that during each year you have 180,000 new readers who have not seen your ad before.

Most newcomers to mail order are tempted to buy ads in an indiscriminate fashion, partly out of confusion and partly out of the belief that spreading their ads around will hasten their success. If you are facing such a temptation, try to resist it. On the basis of what you already know about mail order, and what you have been told about ads, you can see that it would be wiser to buy space in several related magazines than to buy an ad in *Time, Sport, Seventeen, Scholastic, Penthouse, Family Circle* and *Bon Appetit.*

After you get your offer worked out and tested, you will, in all probability, want to use as many magazines as you can in order to increase your over-all volume. But don't add new magazines haphazardly.

Chapter 11

How To Choose The "Right" Magazine to Advertise In

Let's suppose that you now have a product (or service) which you think will sell by mail. Let's suppose further that you believe it will sell directly from the ad. And let's go a step further and assume that you have an ad already written which looks like it will really bring home the bacon. Where do you run the ad?

If these three suppositions are true, you undoubtedly would already have a good idea of where to run the ad. But since this is a hypothetical case, based on a nonexistent product, we can constructively speculate on where the ad should be published.

In determining where to place the ad, we must first ask ourselves some questions about the product itself. To whom does it appeal? Men? Women? Or both? Would it be wanted by sophisticated city-dwellers or by simple rural folk? Is it primarily a gift item or does it serve some instructive or utility purpose? Is it used in the home? The car? The shop? Is it meant primarily for some particular group of tradesmen or professional people—such as Architects? Is its principal appeal one of price, or novelty, or distinctiveness?

These are some of the questions you should ask yourself when you start to advertise a product for sale. In the answers you get will lie the solution to the question, "Which magazine should I advertise in?"

Let's say our mythical product is a new type of fishing lure, that your husband invented. There certainly wouldn't be any problem in determining the medium to be used for this product. You'd use the outdoors magazines, of course, such as

Outdoor Life, Field and Stream, and *Sports Afield.* (The order of listing does not imply any superiority of one over another.)

Or, let's say your product is a bargain package of needles and thread. (Don't sneer. Just such an offer became a tremondous mail order success not too long ago.) Again, there would be no problem. You would use the magazines which are read by women who stay at home: *Ladies Home Journal, Family Circle,* and others. You would not use a magazine read primarily by career women—women to whom home chores are secondary to their jobs. Women of this kind do very little of their own sewing.

Again, suppose your product was a purely masculine product, such as a line of unusual *Genuine Leather Bound Books.* The nature of the product would again dictate the medium to use: magazines that are read by men, men who have the leisure and funds to be rare book collectors. These would be men in an above-average income bracket, as a rule. Which magazine reaches this type of male? There are several: *The Robb Report, Nation's Business, Psychology Today, Smithsonian, Travel Leisure, and Business Week.*

If the product is a utility item for the home or garden, say a set of living room pictures or a new kind of weeding tool, your medium would be in the home-service or shelter publications, such as *House Beautiful, House & Garden,* and *Better Homes & Gardens.*

If the product appeals primarily to some trade, business, or professional group, you would not use the general consumer magazines at all, but rather one or more of the trade journals going directly and exclusively to people in that particular field. Should you take on a line of imported ladies' dinner rings, for example, and want to use the mail order method to wholesale them to jewelers, you would advertise in one of the jewelry trade journals, such as *Jewelers' Circular-Keystone.* If you have an item in the office-supply field, and you want to reach retail dealers with it, there is the trade journal for that field known as *Geyer's Topics.*

Should you formulate and package a line of cosmetics or perfumes, you could get to your market easily enough through the magazines that reach the women who buy products of this kind—the grocery store group, romance group, the confessions group, and the movie magazines. There are dozens of different titles on the newsstands in all three groups.

For a business plan, self-help books, utility gadgets for the shop, and any other items that appeal to the "doers" and "learners," your media would be the mechanics, vocational, and hobby magazines listed in a previous chapter.

If you have a specialty product that you want other salesmen to sell for you, and there is enough profit in it to pay your salesmen a healthy commission and still have some left for yourself, the place to advertise is in the pages of the specialty-selling magazines, *Money Making Opportunities, Spare Time, Entrepreneur, Income Opportunities,* and *Specialty Salesman.* All are very productive pullers for a product with merit.

These illustrations should be sufficient to indicate that the magazine which fits the product and the people who are logical prospects for it. You wouldn't advertise a line of perfumes in the outdoor magazines, or a fishing lure in *Glamour.* Nor would you advertise a set of screwdrivers in *Women's Wear Daily,* or a line of tulip bulbs in *Teen.*

There are many times when your product will be on the borderline, hard to define in terms of exact prospect identity. Take AM FM pocket size Radios. Who buys most of them—men, women or children? Are they bought primarily to use or to give on special occasions? You can't really tell, short of an actual market survey. But surveys are expensive. So the only course open is to use your own judgement plus trial-and-error.

In selecting any medium for advertising your mail order product, there are several important considerations other than the question of whether it fits. One of these is, "Is the magazine I am about to use a 'mail order' magazine?" If you have had much experience with magazines, even as a reader, you will have noticed that some magazines are replete with mail order ads, and that others carry none. There is no easy accounting for this. Why doesn't *Life* carry mail order ads? It ought to, in view of its circulation and the type of people it reaches, but it doesn't.

On the other hand, *The National Enquirer* is a superb mail order medium for dozens of different offers. Why is it so much more widely used than *Life?* They are both sold at the check-out counter of your local food store.

But you don't have to know the "why" of it if you are aware of the curious fact that some magazines are natural mail order mediums and others are not. Your main concern will be in recognizing those which are.

The fact that a magazine is loaded to the brim with mail order ads is irrefutable evidence that that magazine is a good mail order medium. It is that magazine in which you want to advertise. Don't believe the popular fallacy that since a magazine already has so many ads running in it, yours would merely be lost in the shuffle. In point of fact, the reverse is true.

Your ad stands a better chance of paying off when it is placed in proximity to other mail order ads, even though there may be dozens of others surrounding it. Glance at the mail order columns in *Popular Science.* There you see literally hundreds of small ads jammed up tightly against one another—page after page of them. "Who on earth," you ask yourself, "would read my little ad if it were buried among a thousand others?" Plenty of people. One firm recently ran a $142 classified ad in one of the mechanics magazines, and the first insertion of it pulled a thousand inquiries. Had the same ad been placed in a magazine not having many similar mail order ads, it is doubtful that the ad would have been anywhere near as productive as it was.

Another of the important considerations in selecting a medium is to use the one which gives you the most readers per ad dollar. This is where the newcomer often errs, believing that the lowest-cost publication is the cheapest to buy. The reverse is usually true. A simple illustration will prove this: Is it cheaper to pay twenty-five cents per word for an ad in a magazine which has 200,000 reachers, or seventy-five cents a word in one which has two million readers? You don't need a slide rule to work that one out. The seventy-five-cent-per-word medium is the cheaper, even though it calls for a larger cash outlay. That's because you get ten times as many readers for only three times the cost.

Whenever you select a potential ad medium, put it to the test just outlined. Don't think in terms of how many dollars are involved, but only in terms of how many readers you get per dollar. Then buy the one that gives you the most for your dollars.

You may recall that in an earlier chapter I stated that, reader for reader, newspapers are very expensive to use for mail order advertising. That is because newspapers, as a whole, cost an excessive amount per reader when measured against magazines. You pay much more for newspaper ads than you do for national magazine ads. *Unless you buy the space R.O.P.* The most expensive newspaper space of all is in the small town daily or weekly. Consider your *Home Town County Paper,* for example. It has a circulation of maybe ten or twenty thousand. A classified ad in it cost $.15 cents per word. To get some idea of how high this rate actually is, assume that the circulation of this paper suddenly went to a million or two million and the ad rate went up proportionately. You would then be paying $15 to $30 per word for the same ad! The best classified media in the country cost only about one-tenth as much.

The practice of buying the most readers for each ad dollar is especially important when you are using classified ads only. Whereas a display ad might pay out in a low-circulation, high-reader-cost medium, a classified almost never will, particularly if it asks for any kind of remittance. Further, a classified ad is greatly handicapped by its inconspicuous and lack of attention-getting devices. To overcome its handicaps, a classified must be placed where it is exposed to great numbers of readers. The mechanics magazines, as well as some of the mass-circulation grocery store newspapers, make it possible for the small-budget advertiszer to put her message where the odds are very much in her favor. Readership of at least two of the mechanics magazines is around the four million mark, and you can buy classifieds in these publications for a comparatively low amount, about $1.56 per word.

The usefulness of the classified ad is quite limited except as a means of pulling inquiries. As an inquiry-getter, it can and often does work extremely well. If your subsequent sale is sufficiently large, the cost of getting the inquiry through classifieds is negligible. If I were forced to prescribe the best all-around method of making mail sales that a beginner could start with, it would be the inquiry follow-up method, using classified ads to pull inquiries and good follow-up letters to close the sales. But, as qualified earlier, the use of this method depends on what you are selling.

This book won't go into the details of making up a classified ad, except to point out that you should avoid asking your reader for a remittance of any kind. To do so will greatly reduce the number of inquiries you receive, and the quarters and dollars that many such ads ask for do not begin to cover your ad costs except in rare cases. If you are prepared to follow up your inquiries with good sales literature, by all means offer "complete information free." Why should an inquirer send you a quarter to find out what it is you have for sale?

There is one exception to the above remarks. That is when you are using a "leader" as a means of preselecting your prospects to prepare them for a much larger sale. A leader, in mail order parlance, is an item that has value in itself but is used to get high-grade inquiries and weed out curiosity seekers. It usually sells for a very small sum, perhaps a dollar, rarely more, and is directly related to an item of much larger price which you hope to sell to the leader buyer.

For example, if you are offering a book of business plans for $20, you might single out one or two of the better plans, put them into a separate booklet, and offer them as a leader, through classified ads, for one dollar. Then, to the persons who order the one dollar leader booklet, you send the follow-up mailing offering the complete book of plans for $20. The same leader principle can be adapted to nearly any kind of offer, and is a very productive and dependable method of selling by mail.

Chapter 12

The "Time Change" Is The Key To Big Profits

Mail order, like most other fields of business, has certain seasonal characteristics. There are seasons when some mail order products sell like wildfire, and others when they are completely dormant.

For the general run of mail order offers, late fall is the time when sales begin to flow heavily, and they increase steadily through midwinter. They continue at a good rate through winter and early spring, and then subside quickly. Through early and middle summer activity is at a lull.

As a mail order operator, you will want to take advantage of this rise and fall of sales activity, capitalizing on the peak months by doing your heaviest advertising during them.

How the seasons will affect your particular product depends entirely on the product, of course, so you should take the above remarks subject to qualification.

The seasonal aspect of mail order is not inconsistent with what was stated earlier about ad repetition. It only means that after discovering the length of the season for your product, you be repetitious within the season. You would not want to repeat an ad during the off-season just to satisfy the need for repetition, but you can and should repeat your ads as often as possible during the eight or nine months of the normal mail order season. Also, after finding out which of the season's months are your peak months, you will find it profitable to run extra ads during those months.

Products vary a great deal in the extent to which they are affected by the seasons. Items which are designed and sold primarily as gifts sell best during October and the first two weeks in November. (Orders that come in later than that cannot usually be filled and returned to the customer by Christmas Day.) If you were to handle such gift items, you would want to place your heaviest advertising in the October and November issues of the chosen media (*Note:* November issues are usually in readers' hands by the 10th of November, to give them time to make their Christmas purchases and assure them of pre-Christmas delivery.)

On the other hand, if you were selling fishing gear, your best advertising season would begin in February and run through June. If you handled garden tools or other items for outdoor living, your season would begin in early spring and end in midsummer, with perhaps an additional spurt of sales activity in the early fall.

There are some products which are affected by the seasons to only a minor degree. Products in the income opportunity field, for example, often enjoy steady year-round sales, with the summer making only a slight ripple in the sales volume. Such items as office supplies, specialty printing, franchise ads, and other business services usually suffer very little seasonal diminution.

Similarly, books and plans on diets do not undergo such an extreme ebb and flow of sales as do gift items and other consumer products. Most firms that sell plans on how to lose weight keep their advertising programs going full blast from January through November. The same is true of vitamin ads.

Books designed to entertain rather than instruct sell slowly during the warm months but pick up speed rapidly as winter approaches. This is true whether they are sold by direct mail or direct from ads. Self-help books are not so seriously affected.

If you are on the mailing lists of any of the book clubs or popular magazines, you probably have noticed that you receive most of their sales letters and other promotional efforts during October, and January. If you are on the mailing lists of companies selling books and courses of a how-to nature, you are likely to receive their offers any time of the year.

In the final analysis, there is only one way to find out what the seasonal characteristics of a specific product are, and that way is to *test*. The foregoing information is meant to serve as a general guideline, but it will not replace the testing that you eventually will have to do.

Remember, your mail order career will be one of endless testing. Testing for product, testing for method, testing of medium, and now, testing for season. There is no way you can avoid testing in mail order. About the best you can do is to narrow the odds against you by intelligent analysis beforehand, prior to the actual tests, but this merely reduces the risk—it doesn't eliminate the necessity for testing.

Best months in mail order by popular opinion, in descending order:
January, February, October, November, August, September, December, March, April, May, July, and June last.

Chapter 13

The "Magic" Of Legerdemain

If you have ever done any personal selling, you know how difficult it is to go out with your sample case under your arm, stop the first likely-look prospect you run into, and try to interest her in your offer. Chances are that such a "cold" prospect would brush you off forthwith, or at best, start showing you the door about thirty seconds after you had said hello.

But, on the other hand, if you're sitting at home in the evening and a stranger comes to your door and says, "Say, I heard you were selling a line of Ladies' Watches, and I'd like to look them over," your chances of selling this "hot" prospect are extremely good.

The difference between calling on a cold prospect and having a hot prospect call on you is the difference between selling direct from the ad and selling by inquiry follow-up. When you use the inquiry follow-up method, you deal with relatively hot prospects. Inquirers are prewarmed prospects, and they have come to you with their minds already open to receive the details of your *leader offer and future offers*. Whether they buy or not depends entirely on you and the power of your sales literature.

It's no feat of magic to get inquiries. Offer free information on any worthwhile product or offer, and you'll get barrels of inquiries, provided your ad makes the offer sound interesting enough. But changing these inquiries into sales requires a good deal of selling legerdemain.

To convert a satisfactory number of inquiries into sales requires that you not only have a good product at a fair price, but—most important—the kind of follow-up material that makes your prospects want to buy it.

Most inquiry follow-ups use the standard format outlined in a preceding chapter, i.e., sales letter, circular, order form, and reply envelope. If you follow this format for a majority of products, you won't usually go wrong. (There are many other formats and follow-up devices, but these *exotica* are developed and used by firms with years of mail selling experience.)

Second in importance to the standard follow-up format is the old mail order stand-by, the booklet. This is particularly useful in selling items in the higher-price bracket or items that require a lot of explanation.

One woman started out selling a product of her own manufacture using the standard format. It worked very well, resulting in the conversion of about twenty percent of her inquiries into sales. After using this technique awhile, she discovered that there was one dominant element in her sales literature that was mainly responsible for the closing of her sales. Written into her sales letter was a brief dramatic episode in which she narrated the experience of a user in an extremely interesting manner. After learning that it was this paragraph that was doing the most to stimulate sales, she decided that if a little was good, a lot would be even better. So she had her ad agency prepare a new follow-up piece—a thirty-six page booklet— which dramatized every aspect of the product just as she had been doing in the sales letter. The booklet was one long-running narrative about the product: how it was conceived, how it was tested and proved in the field, how it met with instant success among users, and the reports users had sent in after trying it, as well as a biography of the woman who had invented the product to begin with.

A test mailing was made of the booklet, in place of the standard follow-up, and the percentage of sales conversion rose from twenty percent to approximately forty percent. The old follow-up was then scrapped.

This unusual, and irregular booklet violated several mail order principles or at least gave them a terrific warping. Instead of dealing in terms of what the product would do for the customer, it took her on a written tour of the product's history and development...but this history was so dramatized that it was continuously interesting, and apparently gave the prospect a chance to identify with the woman who had originated and sold the idea. By the time the prospect got to the last page of the booklet, she was completely sold, however indirectly the job had been done.

The elements of your follow-up should be as good as you and your copywriter know how to make them. In this connection, don't attempt to write and lay out your own follow-up pieces unless you have had a great deal of mail order experience. It is far less expensive in the long run to have a professional do it for you. (You can find the names and addresses of these people in the mail order trade journals, such as *Direct Marketing* and *DM News.*

If you have had no experience in writing advertising copy, it won't pay you to experiment at the expense of sales. Bad copy can cost you thousands of dollars a year in business you *didn't* get. The difference between bad copy and good copy is very great, although hard to discern beforehand. One particular individual might not be able to see any difference, but the difference will show up drastically when you place the ad in front of thousands of readers of a magazine. A good copywriter knows that on some people who read it, his copy will make no impression whatever. He also knows that his copy will have the opposite effect on a profitable number of readers, and that is the result you are both shooting for.

If you must develop your own follow-up material, however, there is one sure way to do it with the least amount of creative struggle and sales risk. The method works as follows: Having decided what you are going to sell by the inquiry follow-up technique, you search several magazines until you find another firm that is already selling a product similar in nature to yours. Then you determine whether this firm is successful or not by finding out how long it has been advertising and using its present follow-up material.

Your next step is to send an inquiry to this firm asking for free literature. Having it at hand, you study it, analyze it, and parallel it in terms of your own product. Be careful not to pirate, or plagiarize, anything belonging to the other firm. But paralleling is permissible. It's done all the time, even by professionals who don't need to take this kind of short cut.

About the only things that are not freely paralleled and imitated are patented and copyrighted items, trademarks, and things so protected.

You can learn a great deal about developing follow-ups by using the parallel procedure just described. If possible, try to locate not just one but several firms selling products similar to yours, and take a look at their literature, also. From a variety of such literature, you can soon deduce the similarities that are common to all and pinpoint those specific features which you need to parallel in your own material.

Aside from having the best possible sales copy in your follow-up mailing, there are several additional things you can do to stimulate your sales to inquirers. One of the most important is to answer an inquiry as soon as possible after you receive it. Don't wait a day or two; certainly you wouldn't wait a week or more before sending the information your prospect asked for. Remember, she was warmed up at the time she sent her card or letter requesting more information, and she will remain warm just long enough for your letter to reach her by return mail. If she has to wait longer, she starts to cool rapidly. She becomes annoyed and offended that you care so little about her as to delay your response. She soon adopts the attitude that if you are not interested in making a sale to her, she is most certainly not interested in buying your product.

Another important point, touched on earlier in the book, is to make it easy for your prospect to order. Always include an order form and reply envelope (preferably the business-reply postage-paid kind) in your mailings. Keep the order form as simple and explicit as you can. Leave plenty of room for your buyer to write in her name and address, and indicate where to do so. Have spaces for entering the amount of money she is remitting with the order, and the form it takes—whether cash, money order, or check. Bear in mind that she is sending her own money away, and she wants to feel as secure as possible about doing it. Don't ask her to pay her own postage. The lack of a stamp has been the death of many a sale.

The use of a business-reply postage-paid envelope can boost your percentage of sales two percent or more. Think what this would mean on the basis of a thousand inquiries. If you normally close twenty percent of them, an extra two percent would be twenty extra orders—at no extra sales cost.

In connection with follow-ups, you probably have wondered what is the "average" percentage of sales closed to a given number of inquiries. There is no definite answer to this. Some firms feel they are doing well if they convert ten percent of their inquiries into sales. Others are happy with five percent. Still others need fifteen percent to break even. There have been cases of firms closing fifty percent or more of their inquiries, but these are the exceptions by far. The only thing you have to be concerned with is converting enough of the inquiries to yield you a worthwhile profit over and above your product, advertising, and follow-up costs.

Chapter 14

"D M" Can Make You A Millionaire In Six Months

Direct mail is used in many ways. New mothers use it to announce births. Charities use it to solicit money. Creditors use it to send bills. Debtors use it to send excuses. Lovers use it to exchange romantic notes. And politicans use it to stir up votes.

But mail order people use it to make money; *Big Money.*

You, too, can make *Big* money by direct mail by meeting three or four conditions. One, you have to have something good to sell. Two, you have to have a mailing piece that will sell it. Three, you have to have the names and addresses of the people who are prospects for it. And, four, you have to have a lot of these names and addresses.

Direct mail is that simple—or that complicated. If you're experienced with it, you know it is that complicated. If it looks that simple to you, you may approach it with complete self-assurance and faith and proceed to make a fortune. It has been done, and in all probability will be done again.

Getting into direct mail is easy. You locate a product or service having the mail order characteristics previously mentioned. After studying it awhile, you conclude that it would not be suitable for direct-from-ad or inquiry follow-up selling. So you decide that direct mail is the logical method.

Having made this decision, you will roughly follow the procedure that has been followed countless of times by hundreds of direct-mail sellers. Probably the first thing you'll do is sit down at the typewriter and write a sales letter. (This may not be the first thing you do, but it's as good a place to start as any.) Now if you deliberately sit down at the typewriter to compose a sales letter, you will probably write a stinkeroo that wouldn't sell rifles to revolutionists.

But if, on the other hand, you forget all the formidable and formal rules you have ever read about writing sales letters, and instead, sit down and write a polite, well-reasoned letter to a specific person asking her to buy your product, you will probably end up with a gem of a selling letter. If, in attempting to write the letter yourself, you sit and squirm self-consciously at the typewriter without getting anything concrete down on paper, then the best thing for you to do is to forget about writing the letter yourself and turn it over to a professional copywriter. There are some good ones scattered around the country who will charge you a modest fee, *$3,000 to $7,000 for the good ones,* for their services, but their work will be well worth it.

However, if you're persistent, you'll write that sales letter if it kills you. Such tenacity deserves an assist, and here's one in the form of a suggestion: When you start to write your sales letter, go to some of your favorite magazines and take out a picture of one of your favorite people one who is of the same sex and economic circumstances as the typical prospect for your offer and tack this picture to the wall behind your typewriter, where you can see it as you type.

Having put the picture up on the wall where it can be seen, begin your letter and write it as a *personal* one to the character you see in the picture. Forget all about people; instead, write your letter to this one particular person. By this procedure you will almost always write a better letter—one that is convincing and sincere, as well as enthusiastic.

Now in writing the letter to sell your product, it will occur to you as you go along from paragraph to paragraph that there are many things you can tell the prospect, but if you try to tell them all in this letter, it will be far too long to read. So it dawns on you that many of the things that should be said can be left out of the letter and put on a separate piece of paper. After all, you're writing what amounts to a personal letter, and you don't want to bore your reader with too many details—but you don't want to leave them out either. So you collect all these extra details and bits of information about the product and put them in "circular" form, to be mailed along with your letter. It also occurs to you that your prospect might be interested in a picture of the product, so you plan on putting it in the circular, too.

At this point, you are working on two different things at once: a sales letter and a circular. Unless you are unusual, you will probably be a bit confused as to which things go into which of the two pieces. Here is a simple rule of thumb: In the letter you tell your prospect what your product *does* (for her). In the circular you tell her what your product *is*. In the letter you talk benefits and advantages. In the circular, you describe physical features and characteristics.

Assuming that you have now written your letter and circular, and are secretly pleased with your handiwork, the next step in your direct-mail procedure is to go to a printer. You do this because you want these pieces produced in quantity. It occurred to you as you were typing that you were typing on *one* letter to *one* prospect, and if you sent just this one letter out, that particular prospect might not want to buy. So you said to yourself, "Instead of sending just one letter, I'll send a thousand. Out of that many, somebody is sure to buy my product!"

So you take your typewritten copy to a printer and tell him to make you a thousand of each one—letter and circular. And since the letter is a more or less personal one, even though it is to be mailed to a thousand people, you tell him to make it look as much like a typewritten letter as possible. The circular can be printed in the regular way. (*Note:* There are several different processes for turning out sales letters that look as much like individually typed letters as possible. The best—and most expensive—is autotyping, which usually is prohibitive in cost for mass mailings. In terms of looks and cost the two best ones are Laser Printing and offset printing. Your printer can explain the difference.)

While you're at the printer's, you also order a thousand envelopes to mail your letter and circular out in, and a thousand reply envelopes to get the orders back in. (Nope, you won't get a thousand orders back, but you have to send out that many reply envelopes.) You also have him print you a thousand order forms.

A few days later the printer calls you and says your stuff is ready. You rush eagerly to pick it up, and carry the bundles back to your home or office. Spreading the various pieces out on the floor or a kitchen table, you start to collate the pieces.Collating simply means taking one of each of the pieces that go into the envelope and inserting them into it. About midnight you will have gotten all the letters, circulars, etc. into the envelopes, sealed them, put stamps on them, and will be ready to take them to the post office. Bright and early the next morning you do just that.

About four days later the suspense has become unbearable. You have watched for the postman day after day, and each delivery has brought no orders in familiar reply envelopes. Then, on the fifth day, you get an order—and you're walking around on Cloud Nine. The next day five orders come in, and you know you've struck it rich. But then the next day...and the next...and the next...nothing happens. Two weeks later a couple of orders come straggling in, but by then your disappointment is so great that they no longer give you joy.

It's incredible. You mailed a thousand letters and got only eight orders. How could that be possible? You simply can't imagine what went wrong, but if you're made out of good mail order stuff, you'll jolly well set about finding out!

It is at this point that you really begin to understand direct mail. You can read all the books in the library on the subject, and they won't mean as much to you as the experience I've just described. (Strictly a hypothetical example, oversimplified to give you a quick capsule sketch of a typical beginner's entree into direct mailing.) Direct mail is like swimming or piloting an airplane: You can't fully learn it without actually jumping in and doing it. This is no argument against reading books on the subject. By all means do so; the more the merrier. But don't expect the books to take the place of a good dose of experience; on the contrary, it is usually after you've gotten your feet good and wet that the books begin to make sense and become of real help. Because by then you can relate what you read to your own tangible experience.

There is only one way to get into direct mail, and that way is to hit on a product or service that looks good (in terms of the previously listed mail order requirements), and roughly following the procedure outlined in this chapter, give it a test. The test mailing will give you a feel of direct mail and will help you decide in which direction to go beyond that. If the test is successful, then you continue mailing at the same or an increased rate; if it fails, you look for another offer and try again.

You'd be perfectly justified in saying that the preceding capsule version of the direct-mail business is not a particularly appetizing or encouraging one, not at all the kind of thing you're used to reading and hearing about. If it sounds that way to you, please understand that my purpose in so presenting it has been to impress upon you the fact that direct mail does involve a high element of risk, especially at the start, and unless you are willing and able to afford the risk, it might be wise for you to use one of the other two methods in the beginning.

There is an optimistic side, however. That is that a great deal of money is being made by many different firms who operate strictly by direct mail, and the odds are even that if you try long enough, hard enough, and intelligently enough, you can be one of them.

For the newcomer, direct mail should serve primarily as an adjunct to direct-from-ad or inquiry follow-up selling. If you sell from ads, you can test direct mail, on a small scale, as you go along, being careful not to let it siphon off funds that you need for the normal operation of your direct-from-ad business. It is easy to acquire some name lists from outside sources and send your mailing pieces to these prospects. Should small-scale tests then indicate that direct mail is your most profitable method of doing business, you could wisely drop the other methods and devote all your efforts to this one.

Numerous products lend themselves to profitable direct-mail selling. Current direct-mail sellers are real estate books, stock market manuals, money making books, insurance, newsletters, electronic catalogs, women's catalogs, women's sports, jewelry, imported foods, nursery items, and dozens of others. (If you are not now receiving a good many direct-mail offers, it will pay you to get your name on some lists and start receiving them.)

In anything that is successfully sold by direct mail, there will always be certain peculiar characteristics. One of these is the average unit of sale. It almost never will be under $20. It is next to impossible to sell anything by direct mail for less than this amount and make a profit. This fact is attributable primarily to the high costs of printing, postage, and labor—all of which have a steady trend upward. So as you go about selecting something to offer by this method, bear the price consideration in mind. Keep it at $20 or more. The ideal price for a direct-mail item is probably $24.95 or slightly below.

Another outstanding quality of successful direct mail offers is uniqueness. Examine a dozen different propositions, and you will find that there will be something definitely unique about each one. The product itself may not be unique, but it will have unique features of function or design. Or it may be a run-of-the-mill product which carries a uniquely attractive price. Or, in another instance, it may be a standard product which carries with it a unique premium offer. But in all cases, whatever the product, the offer will have something unique or different about it to distinguish it from other direct-mail offers and to differentiate it from similar goods sold in stores.

A third quality of a good direct-mail proposition is that it be something which is *something* that leads to another sale in the future. As in selling direct from the ad, you cannot thrive in direct mail on customers that buy just one time. You must sell them a second time, and keep on selling them, whether you sell them more of the same item or something that is different yet related to the first item. Ideally, *something* that is used up by the customer quickly, and she sends in an order for more of the same without further solicitation or sales cost. Thus, the second order contains a long, clean profit, unburdened by any further mailing or effort outside of filling the order. This kind of repeat potential is present in all successful direct-mail sellers. If the product you select is not in itself susceptible to being used up, then you must look around for a similar item that you can sell to the people who buy the first one. For example, a firm that sells beauty products generates its repeat business through the sale of cosmetics and other beauty supplies. If it were to sell one product only, it would not have a very profitable operation.

In direct mail your profit almost never will be in making that first sale but in making subsequent sales. The profit is there to be made after you have built up a good list of customers, because it is much easier to sell to them the second time. For instance, a firm dealing in cheese realizes about a three percent return from its first "cold mailing" to housewives. Out of a million letters mailed, the firm accumulates thirty thousand customers. A lot of customers, but not very much profit. But this firm then sends out a mailing to these customers after an interval, and realizes nearly a twenty percent response. In the twenty percent response, there is a very substantial profit; in fact, the profit from mailing to their thirty thousand customers is greater than their profit in mailing one million cold letters.

Another feature of a good direct-mail offer is that it rarely ever asks for a remittance in advance. It has been found that the number of orders received from a mailing can be increased considerably by offering to ship on approval or on open account. It has also been found that while shipping on such terms can raise the response a great deal, the credit loss is not raised proportionately. Most people, it is true, are honest. If they receive a satisfactory product which lives up to its original advertising claims, they will pay for it. Naturally, you will run into some professional dead beats who won't pay for the goods, but these are in the minority and a small price to pay for the large increase in volume of orders you can usually expect by offering to ship on approval or credit. (It is taken for granted, of course, that you would preselect your prospects by financial or economic standing in order to make certain that they have the money to buy what you have to offer. Mailing-list counselors can be invaluable in helping you select lists of prospects who are financially responsible.)

These, then, are the main characteristics of a good direct-mail offer: a price of $20 or more, repeat potential, uniqueness of product or offer, and liberal selling terms. That a product embodies all these features does not guarantee its success, of course. Other matters will have their effect also: the quality of the lists you use, the impressiveness of your mailing, the season and timing. But it can safely be said that if an offer does *not* possess these main characteristics, it is not likely to sell profitably by direct mail.

In discussing the qualities of a direct-mail product, no mention was made of two other important features which by now should be an integral part of your mail order thinking.

One, the product should have a long profit margin, and two, the product must be guaranteed. Most direct-mail products have a profit ranging from fifty to eighty percent. The longer the profit, the better off you are. Don't feel guilty about making a long profit on a worthwhile product. You'll need every bit of your margin to cover your costs, expand your mailings, and yield a profit for yourself.

The matter of guarantees is a special one and will be dealt with in a later chapter. At this point, it suffices to say that you must guarantee your product in mail order and live up to your guarantee. Nothing will help you make sales faster or create more satisfied customers. Nothing will make customers angrier and cause you to lose them faster than not living up to your guarantee.

No discussion of direct mail would be complete without a statement of what you can expect in the way of response to your mailings. There is no definite answer to this, except that it nearly always is less than you think it will be. Some firms get by with fewer orders per thousand letters than others. Magazines, as a rule, can afford to accept a response of two percent because of their high percentage of renewals in future years. Specialized mailings to special groups of prospects may produce orders to the extent of five percent or so. General consumer mailings rarely exceed a four percent response. A "teaser" mailing, offering a free gift or premium only, may pull as high as forty to fifty percent. In general, if you sell a product in the $20 to $30 range, in which you have a seventy percent profit margin, and you pull three percent in orders, you are doing very well—probably above average.

Chapter 15

The Sales Letter Can Make You Or Break You

The best way to write a sales letter is to hire a professional copywriter. The next best way is to do it yourself.

In mail order you nearly always need one or more sales letters. In inquiry follow-up and direct mail the letter is the soul of your business. It is more important than any piece you send out, although this statement may precipitate some dispute among other mail order people. It is the letter that ultimately sways your prospect for or against your offer and causes her to buy or not to buy.

There is an astounding difference between a good sales letter and a bad one. Although, as in display ads, the difference may be hard to detect in advance, it shows up in a very dramatic way in the number of orders pulled. A good letter often will do five or ten times the business that a poor one does. The only way to find out which is which is by testing.

There are many ways to go about writing a sales letter. Every writer has her own method, her own set of psychic conditions; and don't feel badly if, in sitting down to write your letter, you feel that you haven't made quite the right preliminary motions. It doesn't matter how you approach the task; you can write your letter in longhand or in Sanskrit, while in bed or hanging from the parallel bars. Just so you get it down on paper and it sells.

To write a sales letter to sell a product, you must first have the product. Now if you have the product, or a sample of it, set it on your desk alongside of your typewriter. Next, crank a blank sheet of paper into your typewriter. Then conjure up a mental image of a particular person to whom you think you can sell this particular product. (If your cerebellum screen is a little snowy, turn it off and follow the method given in the last Chapter.

Now you have the perfect setting in which to compose a sales letter. You have the prospect in your head or on the wall; you have the product on the desk beside you; and you have the means of communicating the sales message in your typewriter.

All you have to do now is convince the character in your mind that she needs and must have the product on your desk. Whether you succeed or not depends entirely on the words you select and the order in which you line them up.

That is about all anybody can tell you about how to write a sales letter. True, you can buy dozens of books on the subject; you can go to night school and hear lecturers describe various sure-fire techniques; you can take correspondence courses in copywriting. But none of these activities will equip you to write a particular sales letter to sell your particular product. From the moment you hit the first typewriter key, you discover that you are strictly on your own, and all the rules and tricks you've learned will not do the writing for you.

There is, of course, the standard sales formula to which any finished sales letter must conform. It is: *attention, interest, desire, exclusive,* and *action.* A good letter will contain all the elements of this formula. Take the first one, *attention.* You know beforehand that to get a prospect to read your letter, you must first get her attention. If you don't grab her attention quickly, into the wastebasket goes your letter. So you put something in the letter that will catch her eye, that will stop her from whatever else she is thinking about and cause her mind to focus on what *you* have to say. This "something," normally called the headline, goes at the top of your letter, where it will be seen before the rest of the copy.

Your attention-getter is very important. It must not only get your prospect's attention, but it must lead logically into the main portion of your letter. The best attention-getter is one that grows out of your product and contains your essential sales appeal.

Attention-getters that are built in, or derived from the product itself are the best. However, you can't always be lucky enough to have such a custom-built opener. In its absence, you can usually rely on one of the stock openers.

You've seen many of them in letters you've received in the past. They are identified by such words as "New!" "At Last!" "Now!" "Free!" "You Are Invited To Accept...."

These are a few of the standardized openings you'll find in hundreds of different sales letters. They aren't copyrighted; you can take any one of them and adapt it to fit your letter. You can find many more good attention-getters just by examining the direct-mail offers you get in your daily mail. (In fact, these are the best possible examples you can use, and because they are a common part of every office and household, I have not used space here to reproduce any of them.)

If you aren't receiving any direct-mail offers, by all means, subscribe to a couple of magazines or buy something else by mail that will automatically get your name on some mailing lists. If you get on one or two, you will soon be on a dozen or more and start receiving offers of all kinds. That's because mailing-list houses sell the customer lists of one firm to many other firms.

All good attention-getters embody news, intrigue, shock, or unusual information. Put any of these elements into your headline and you're bound to get attention. Everybody is interested in something "new." If you have a new product, or one which is new to the prospect, include the news angle in your opener.

Intrigue is good if it is carefully handled. Here's a good example: "$25,000 Dollars For A Few Hours Work Doesn't Seem Fair!..." Now *there* is an opener! It would be hard to resist finding out what this "system" is, almost impossible to keep from reading the rest of the letter.

Shock is sure to get attention, but it must be the right kind of shock. Not the kind you create by yelling "Fire!" in a crowded theatre. A fine example is the one contained in a letter sent to businessmen by a prominent insurance company. It said, "If you died tonight, would your wife be able to operate your business..." And then the story led into the need of a man in business for himself to protect those who would not be able to step into his shoes. The letter sold a lot of insurance.

Not only your opener but the entire letter should stress those things which will be of selfish interest to your prospect.

101

You never write your letter around *your* reasons for wanting her to buy your product—instead, you concentrate on *her* reasons for buying it. You don't write to a prospect and say, "Look, Joan, I want you to buy this Watch because I am trying to get a new car and it will help me if you buy the Watch." Such a plea might elicit a little sympathy, but it won't get you a new car. Instead, you say, "I want you to buy this Watch because it will make you more attractive to men...help you get a raise...make you the envy of the country club set..." and so on. See the difference?

In this discussion of the composition of sales letters, it is assumed that you have a passing knowledge of business letters and the usual form they take. If you don't, hunt up a textbook on business correspondence and relearn how to write a business letter. The only difference between a conventional business letter and a direct-mail sales letters is the *purpose*. A sales letter is meant to get orders. With one or two exceptions, the form is the same as that followed by any business letter.

Whereas a business letter opens with the name and address of the person to whom you're writing and includes a salutation, most mail order sales letters nowadays do away with these items completely, because it is not economically feasible in most mass-mailing operations to fill them in. *(Except with laser printing.)*

Just as most sales letters dispense with a formal salutation, they also omit the nauseating familiar "Dear Friend" that used to be used so regularly. Many people resent being called "Dear" and "Friend," especially by someone at a remote distance who has no right to presume such a relationship.

The other essential difference between a business letter and a sales letter is the one previously discussed—the attention-getter, headline, opener, or whatever you choose to call it. This usually takes the form of two or three double-spaced typewritten lines (often indented or staggered) above the main body of the letter, where the salutation normally is situated.

There are two general ways to get attention in sales-letter copy. One is to make a statement; the other is to ask a question. If you make a statement, it should contain something that is new, different, or interesting. If you ask a question, ask one which cannot be answered immediately with a Yes or No; or if it does call for a spontaneous answer, be sure the answer is Yes, so as to put the prospect into an affirmative frame of mind for the rest of the message.

Here are several tips on writing effective headlines:

Begin your headline with the word "New" or "Now."
Begin your headline with the words "At Last!"
Begin your headline with "How" or "How To,"
Begin your headline with the word "Which."
Talk about money in your headline...in dollars and cents
Use the word "Free."
Use the word "Amazing."
Use The Word "You."

Once you have thought out a suitable headline for your sales letter, one that will get attention from your reader, your next step is to convert this *attention* into *interest*. This is most often done by elaborating or explaining the headline.

From that point on, the rest is easy. The letter continues to describe the product in terms which will make the reader want to buy it; in other words, *desire.* And if the desire is fired to the proper temperature, the final element of our formula, *action,* will be forthcoming. Because if you make a person *want* a product more than she wants the money she is being asked to part with, she'll buy it.

There are several ways to go about putting desire-inducing elements into your sales letter. But as in writing the letter, all this instruction can do is provide a method or formula...it cannot do the actual work for you.

The best approach is to take a sample of your product and put it on your desk or in some other spot where you can see it, handle it, smell it, measure it, taste it, and weigh it. Then, with pen and paper or typewriter make as comprehensive a list as you possibly can of all the positive qualities of the product, beginning with those you think are most appealing, and ending with the least important ones.

Once you have such a list of qualities or features, you simply proceed to turn each listed quality into a "selling phrase."

Suppose it is made of strong plastic—not a very startling fact, but one which under many circumstances could be turn-

ed into a selling phrase or sentence by pointing up the sales features of this peculiar plastic itself. Here is an example: "Durably constructed of finest plastic to assure you of long rust-free, break-free life!"

This is a prosaic example, to be sure, but you can see the moral. *Any* product can be skillfully turned into a selling phrase if you work at it a little. (This includes the *bad* qualities!)

Once you have itemized the qualities of your product and turned them into the best selling phrases of which you are capable, your next step is to write your letter in such a manner that it incorporates—in an easy-to-read, fluid sequence— all the phrases you've devised.

If you have done a good job of it up to this point, you have probably succeeded in arousing some degree of desire in your prospect, and the next stage is to solidify this desire by demonstrating that what you have told him is true.

The matter of *proof* is important to an effective sales letter, and should be built into every letter you use. Its most popular form is the testimonial from a satisfied user. (It is no trick to get all the good testimonials you can use; all you need do, after you have sold a number of your products, is write to your customers and ask them to give you their personal opinions and experiences with the product. A surprising number of your customers will be more than glad to do this.)

Other forms of proof are specific statements of value, as supported by manufacturers' literature, research reports, and statements by recognized authorities.

When you reach the end of your letter, after the proof, it is time to push for some kind of action. The simplest and most fundamental action-getter is to flatly ask for an order. Ask your prospect to buy and to buy now—today—without delay. If possible, give her reasons for avoiding delay. If there is a limited supply, tell her so. If you are offering a bargain price that will soon go up, tell her that. If the offer has a logical time limit on it, state it in a specific number of days.

Any legitimate means by which you can push your prospect into ordering *at once* will pay big dividends. People suffer greatly from inertia, and the prospect who was "almost" sold today will be twice as difficult to warm up tomorrow.

In writing your sales letter (or any other mail order copy for that matter), it is always best to use simple words, short phrases, and clear sentences that anyone can understand on the first reading. Don't be ambiguous. Don't use ornate terms or flowery phrases. Stay away from any attempt at phony sophistication or "fine writing"...including precious foreign words that only a college student who majored in Romance Languages could understand.

If you can get by with one vivid word, it isn't necessary to use two weaker ones. It is easy to say to yourself, "Well, a million people are going to read my letter, so what if a few of them don't get the message at first glance?" The best attitude to have (the *only* attitude to have) is to assume that you have only one prospect in the whole wide world, and only one chance to make the sale...and everything hinges on the way you phrase that one letter.

A further suggestion is that you strive for *plausibility* in your letter. It is easy to get so enthused about your product or offer that the copy to sell it comes out wholly unbelievable. Any copy that is destined to pull mail orders will be plausible, will cause your prospect to believe every word you say.

Another suggestion (indeed, an imperative) is that your copy express real sincerity. The absence or presence of sincerity in a letter can quickly be detected by your reader, and can either induce her to buy or cause her to reject the offer as sounding phony.

Sincerity can't be faked with any sustained degree of success. It stems from your own basic belief in yourself and your product. And if you have this belief and faith, the sincerity will shine through all your letters and ads.

Professional copywriters have been known to condescendingly describe the method of building a sales letter outlined here as mechanical or contrived. But if you have never written a sales letter, and you want to learn, this method will help you immensely. Remember, you merely line up your qualities and features, and turn them into selling phrases; then, like a chain of dominoes standing on end, you thump them over. Each one falls into the next, until you have made all your sales points in a smooth, effective manner.

Having used the qualities of your product as a blueprint for constructing your sales letter, you can similarly build in added impact by making a list of all the reasons why your prospect might *not* want to buy the products, and endeavoring to overcome these reasons within the body of the letter... before your reader has a chance to think of them herself, independently.

For instance, your prospect may think the price is too high, or she wants to buy but not just yet. In the first instance, you point out that the price may appear to be high, but when compared to products of a similar kind or of inferior make, it really is an exceptionally low price. Either that or you express the total price in such a way that it seems much lower than it actually is: "Only 30 cents per day pays for this Watch," or "For less than you spend for a newspaper, you can own this handsome new Watch."

If she wants to buy, but not right now, you must put some kind of penalty on waiting. This is easily done by offering her a cash discount for ordering immediately, or by offering a free premium if she places her order within a certain period of time.

Other objections that a prospect can make will occur to you if you make a deliberate effort to study and list the bad or negative qualities of your offer. Write them all down, and then figure out ways to overcome them. There are a dozen objections a prospect can make to buying your product, or reasons she can give for putting off the purchase, and it is your duty to anticipate as many of them as you can—*bring them into the letter*—with corresponding reasons why she should not let these factors interfere with her immediate ownership and enjoyment of your product.

This has been an attempt to show you how to write a sales letter. All it can be is an attempt, because no one can really show you how to do it. The best that can be done is to describe a pattern or formula and make suggestions for following it, as I have done here. This chapter gives you one such formula. It is no better and no worse than a dozen others you will find in textbooks and courses on letter-writing. As stated in the beginning of the chapter, the best way to get a sales letter written is to have it done by a professional copywriter (one who writes *mail order* copy, not the typical ad agency type who suffers for days the creative throes of agonizingly composing a three-line piece for a client in the dry cleaning business).

The next best way is to sit down at the typewriter and do it yourself. In doing it yourself, it doesn't matter whether it comes out good or bad the first time. If you work at it, using this or some other pattern to go by, you're bound to come up with a pretty good letter...probably better than you think. You might even—as has happened repeatedly with people who have never before in their life written a sales letter—come up with the *perfect* letter for your product.

There is one tremendous advantage you have over a professional copywriter: Your product is one which you know personally and are enthusiastic about, and this enthusiasm will frequently make up for any technical deficiencies your letter might have.